John B. Keane is one of Ireland's most humorous authors and is recognised as a major Irish playwright. He has written many bestsellers including *Durango, Letters of a Successful TD, Letters of an Irish Parish Priest, Letters of an Irish Publican, Letters of a Matchmaker, Letters of a Love-Hungry Farmer, The Gentle Art of Matchmaking, Irish Short Stories, Love Bites and Other Stories, The Ram of God and Other Stories, The Bodhrán Makers* and *Man of the Triple Name.* His plays include *The Field, The Year of the Hiker, Moll, Big Maggie, Sive, Sharon's Grave, Many Young Men of Twenty, The Change in Mame Fadden, Values, The Crazy Wall* and *The Buds of Ballybunion.*

# The Man from Clare

A Play in Two Acts by

## John B. Keane

*New Revised Text*
*edited by*
*Ben Barnes*

## THE MERCIER PRESS

The Mercier Press Limited
P.O. Box 5, 5 French Church Street, Cork *and*
24 Lower Abbey Street, Dublin 1

© John B. Keane, 1992


ISBN 1 85635 029 0

A CIP catalogue record for this book
is available from the British Library.

*The Man from Clare* is a copyright play and may not be performed without a licence. Application for a licence for amateur performances must be made in advance to The Mercier Press, P.O. Box 5, 5 French Church Street, Cork. Professional terms may be had from Mr John B. Keane, 37 William Street, Listowel, Co. Kerry.

Music set by Ossian Publications, Cork
Printed in Ireland by Colour Books Ltd.

This revised two act version of *The Man from Clare* was first presented by Groundwork in association with Gaiety Entertainments at the Gaiety Theatre on 30 July 1992.

| | |
|---|---|
| *Packey* | Mark O'Regan |
| *Petey* | Liam Heffernan |
| *Daigan* | Mick Lally |
| *Cooney* | Risteard Cooper |
| *Frank* | Frank O'Sullivan |
| *Jim Flynn* | Conor McDermottroe |
| *Padraic O'Dea* | Brendan Gleeson |
| *Bríd* | Fionnuala Murphy |
| *Nellie Brick* | Ruth McCabe |
| *Morisheen Brick* | Johnny Murphy |
| *Elsie McDonagh* | Marina Ní Dhubhain |
| *A Girl* | Sonja Broderick |
| *Footballers* | Kieran Hurley |
| | Tim Murphy |
| | Andrew Bennett |
| | David Collins |
| | Cormac Costello |
| | Daragh Byrne |

| | |
|---|---|
| *Director* | Pat Laffan |
| *Designer* | Brien Vahey |
| *Lighting* | Rupert Murray |
| *Producers* | Ben Barnes |
| | Arthur Lappin |
| *Executive Producer* | Ronan Smith |

*The Man from Clare* was first produced by the the Southern Theatre Group on 1 July 1962 at the Father Mathew Hall, Cork, with the following cast:

| | |
|---|---|
| *Packey* | Michael Twomey |
| *Petey* | Ber Power |
| *Daigan* | Dan Donovan |
| *Cooney* | Charles Ginnane |
| *Frank* | Pat Duggan |
| *Jim Flynn* | Flor Dullea |
| *Padraic O'Dea* | Michael McAuliffe |
| *Bríd* | Abbey Scott |
| *Nellie Brick* | Máirín Murphy |
| *Morisheen Brick* | James N. Healy |
| *Elsie McDonagh* | Irene Comerford |
| *Other footballers* | Seán Healy |
| | Noel Quinn |

| | |
|---|---|
| *Producer* | Dan Donovan |
| *Scenery* | Frank Sanquest |

# ACT ONE

## Scene 1

*Action takes place in darkness, near the harbour of Cuas on the Clare side of the Shannon River on a May morning, with the dawn no more than minutes away. There is the light of a good moon where men might advance to be seen. A group of men are gathered in the half light, with bundles of football togs. One has a football, and another an accordion. They are the Cuas team from Clare, waiting for the motorboat which will take them across the river to play the annual match against the Bealabawn team from North Kerry. Two raw and awkward young men, Pakey and Petey, are in the centre of the stage. They are argumentative.*

| | |
|---|---|
| **Pakey** | Three years ago, when I was second sub, I was late through no fault of my own and the boat went without me. I was only a minute late and they were only just barely out from the pier at Bealabawn. I roared at them and I yelled at them and I screeched at them but they never put back for me. |
| **Petey** | You were tellin' me that before! |
| **Pakey** | I flung big rockers o' stones after 'em, an' they didn't even look behind. |
| **Petey** | There should be a rule about it! |
| **Pakey** | That's right! A rule is the thing. I'll propose it, if you'll second it. |
| **Petey** | Propose it so! |
| | *(Pakey rises and stands on minor elevation.)* |

**Pakey**     Lads ... lads ... (*The hum of conversation dies.*) I propose a rule.

**Petey**     And I second it.

**Pakey**     Passed.

**Daigan**    What's the rule?

**Pakey**     The rule is that I was left behind three years ago and I was stranded in Kerry for a day and a night all on account of I goin' off with a carload o' girls to a dance in Abbey-feale, and I propose that no one be left behind ever again an' that no man board the boat until every man is accounted for an' that way we'll all arrive home here together an' there'll be no need for awkward explanations to our women. That's the rule!

**Petey**     An' I second it!

**Daigan**    A vote! All in favour say 'Aye!'

              (*A number of 'Aye's are heard.*)

**Daigan**    And now—who's against?

              (*There are no responses.*)

**Daigan**    I see! Well, I'm against an' I'm dead against! I want to hear no more about that. When the boat is ready, we're ready an' any man that's late, we'll go without him, an' on top o' that I'll see that he's suspended for twelve months from the Club. What business have I tryin' to train you to be footballers if you're goin' to be out all night like a squad o' tomcats? The boat will be comin' back here four hours after the match. That's ten o'clock. You'll have four hours for drinkin', or courtin', or fightin', accordin' to your lights. Ten o'clock, I say ... sharp!

| | |
|---|---|
| **Pakey** | Well, I object … are you goin' to second me Petey? |
| **Petey** | Yerra, second yourself! I'm sick o' bein' second. |
| **Voice** | What's for the winners today? |
| **Daigan** | There's a set o' silver medals an' a cup for the Captain, and remember, when you're out on the field, the Captain has the last word. Whatever he says is law. All agree? |

*(Shouts of 'Aye!' 'Proper order!' etc.)*

| | |
|---|---|
| | Now there's one more very important question to be decided before the boat comes, an' that's the question of Captain. I want no say in that, so 'tis up to yourselves. |
| **Voice** | Padraic O'Dea, o' course…! Who else? |
| **Voices** | 'Yes, Padraic O'Dea!' 'A tried man!' etc. |
| **Pakey** | I'm for Padraic O'Dea! |
| **Petey** | And I'm for him, too. |
| **Voices** | 'O'Dea!' 'Padraic O'Dea!' |
| **Voice** | With all due respects and no reflections intended, I think it's about time someone else got a turn. The captaincy should go round. |
| **Voice** | But there's no one as good as Padraic an' we want a good captain. |
| **Voice** | What about Jim Flynn? |
| **Daigan** | Fair enough! For Padraic O'Dea, the Ayes? |
| **Voices** | Aye! |
| **Daigan** | For Jim Flynn? |

*(There is no response.)*

**Jim**  I didn't want to be captain anyway!

**Pakey**  I'd never vote for anyone only Padraic O'Dea.

**Petey**  Me the same!

**Daigan**  Anythin' else on anybody's mind? No good talkin' about these things when we're in the middle o' the Shannon.

**Voice**  If a fellow wanted to bring home a couple o' hundred o' good spuds, would there be room in the boat?

**Daigan**  Out o' the question! I won't have it! The next thing you know some fellow would want to bring home a cock o' hay, or an in-calf heifer.

**Voice**  Or a woman!

**Voices**  Aye!

**Voice**  Lively women in North Kerry!

**Voice**  Who's the referee today?

**Daigan**  He's a man called Driscoll, from Cork.

**Voice**  Couldn't they get anythin' but a Corkman?

**Voice**  Are we to get anythin' out o' the gate?

**Daigan**  They're payin' for the boat an' there's a free feed after the match, an' porter for anyone that wants it. They can't do any more, an' knowin' some o' the porter guzzlers in this team, they'll want a very good gate to pay for it.

**Voice**  Is the team picked?

| | |
|---|---|
| **Daigan** | 'Twas picked last night.... Get up now an gather round and I'll give you your positions. |

*(They gather round Daigan. A man comes from the crowd upstage, into the light, and begins to examine his compact arrangement of football boots, togs and stockings. He kneels while he goes carefully through his gear and calls: 'Padraic! ... Padraic!' to the background of conversation.*

*A man advances from the crowd and stands over him. He too carries football gear.)*

| | |
|---|---|
| **Padraic** | What ails you now? |
| **Jim** | I'm half in dread to tell you! I want to ask you something and I can't get it out of me. |
| **Padraic** | Why did you call me, then...? Don't you know Daigan is advisin' the lads...? Come on! That's where you should be, too, listenin' to Daigan. Japers, man, if we're beat today it's the finish of us! *(Kindlier)* What are you doing out here alone, anyway? |
| **Jim** | I'm in dread ... I'll tell you no lie.... This is my first time playing the other side of the Shannon. I'm in dread of my sacred life of the Kerry lads. 'Tisn't afraid of what will happen to me at all, I am, but 'tis how I'm afraid I'll run an' leave the rest of ye down if there's crossness or boxing. |
| **Padraic** | You're not a coward are you? |
| **Jim** | I'm no coward and I'll hold my own with any fellow, but I'm afraid all the same. |

*(Padraic kneels down.)*

**Padraic**    Of course you are! Every man is a coward until he's cornered. Your courage will surface when the whistle sounds and the ref throws in the ball.

**Jim**    'Tis aisy for you! You're the best man in Clare, Padraic, an' you're afraid of nothin' an' everybody knows you, an' no one will challenge you.

**Padraic**    Look Jim, boy! ... Football is a sport with blood in it, a sport of strength and hard hittin' and fair play: a sport with its own share of blackguards, but they're scarce and most of the lads are the same as ourselves. Look what football is ... 'tis goin' for the ball and doin' your best to get it. If you get a ball 'tis your ball and if a fellow tries to take it from you, take the proper proceedings against him. But never hit a man from behind, never blackguard a man that's weary and played out and, above all, never kick a man whether he's up or down, but if a fellow hits you a lick of an elbow or a belt of his bottom, belt him back or you've no business playin' football.

**Jim**    What about the ref?

**Padraic**    A ref has only two eyes so be your own ref when he can't attend to you.

**Jim**    What's it like over in Kerry?

**Padraic**    Over in Bealabawn, you mean? I don't know. I played there ten times, twelve times. I've half the games forgot. They always beat us on their own sod but we were never cowarded. That's the main thing. Bealabawn! 'Tis only a streel of a village

with two pubs. Come on man, or Daigan
will be like a devil!

Jim

Padraic!

Padraic

What?

Jim

If there's a row today will you back me? ...
Well, will you?

Padraic

If 'tis a fair fight, you'll be on your own,
but if a man is outnumbered or kicked
when he's down, I'll be there ... fair
enough?

Jim

Fair enough!

Padraic

Come on then!

Jim

Would you say there'll be a row today?

Padraic

How do I know? Look ... if a fellow puts a
fight up to you, remember the first clout is
the one that counts. A good early clatter
into the gills and you have a fellow half-
giddy before the fight starts at all.

*(Daigan arrives upstage. He is a man with
wild eyes and a head of wild grey hair.)*

Daigan

Did ye think I was speakin' to myself, or
somethin', back there? Get up! ... In the
honour o' God get up, an' wouldn't ye listen to my plan o' play?

*(Others of the crowd gather nearer.To man in
background)* Take the lantern, Pakey. We'll
go to the boat now.

*(A torch is lighted in background.)*

Once more, lads ... gather up an' sit down.
*(They come around Daigan in a circle.)* Any
free kicks in their half of the field, you take

them, and remember to get your heel back up to your arse when taking a free. If you don't get the heel back up to your arse you won't drive the ball. Did I ever tell you about Long Legs Callaghan from Killishen? Christ there was your kicker of a dead ball! One time they placed the football on a *triopall* of *fionnán* and he stood back from it, cocked his rear, smote it. The cover of that ball landed outside the presbytery in the town of Kilrush and the bladder landed outside the hall door of a whorehouse in Buenos Aires! You're a young team with the exception of Padraic here, an' he's wiser than any o' you. This team you're meetin', Bealabawn, they're crabbed an' crafty, an' they'll have players from all over North Kerry but they'll all be ancient footballers because there's nothin' good comin' up to them. Here's our plan. Hit 'em an' harry 'em an' keep hittin' 'em until they're tired. Wear 'em down first an' then play the ball well to the wings, so that they won't be able to run after it. Then lob the ball into the goals an' every man that's near, in on top of 'em an' no mercy. Are we right?

**Chorus**    Right!

**Daigan**    Who has the jerseys?

**Voice**    They're safe! I have 'em.

**Daigan**    We've nothin' to lose, an' it could be the first time in thirty odd years we beat Bealabawn on their own ground. 'Twould be an awful blow to them an' they always so cocky an' full o' gumption. Lads, we're not representin' Clare here today. We're only a

club team but we are from Clare. I have
seen good Clare teams and bad Clare
teams but I have never seen a Clare team
that was cowardly ... and I don't want to
see one here today.

**Voice**     *(From the distance)* Hi, lads! Come on! The
tide is right an' the engine is runnin'!

**Daigan**    *(Shouts)* Right! ... We'll be with you in a
minute. One more thing, lads ... if it
should happen that we're a few points
ahead towards the end of the match, they'll
do all in their power to start a fight. Don't
hit back if you're winnin'!

**Voice**     What about the referee?

**Daigan**    A Corkman, is it? He'd enjoy nothin' better
than to see Kerry an' Clare fightin'!

*(They rise to their feet. They all stand fervent-
ly to attention. A banner, held by two men, is
visible with the slogan 'COME ON CUAS!'
written on it. They form a sort of company
while a man with a melodeon starts into the
tune of 'The Men from Cuas'. The company
marks time. After a while, still marking time,
they sing 'The Men from Cuas'.)*

**All**       Glory to the men of Cuas
The pride of the County Clare
In the rough or on the loose
The Cuas boys will be there.
Cuas boys here, Cuas boys there
Cuas boys, Cuas boys everywhere.
Cuas, Cuas, Cuas,
Cuas, Cuas, Cuas,
The men of Cuas are always there.

> Now we go to play the game
> To field the dropping ball
> The men from Cuas will play it fair
> Let each man give his all
> Cuas boys here, Cuas boys there
> Cuas boys, Cuas boys everywhere.
> Cuas, Cuas, Cuas,
> Cuas, Cuas, Cuas,
> The men of Cuas are always there.

*(We hear their voices until they fade into silence. Padraic and Daigan are about to follow.)*

**Daigan**      Don't waste yourself in the first half, Padraic. Leave the young lads do the work. Wait till the last quarter an' you'll see gorgeous opportunities. Let yourself go then! Hammer the goals with low balls an' we'll bring the Cup back to Cuas tonight....

**Daigan**      I have a feelin' we'll win today!

**Padraic**      So have I!

**Daigan**      What was wrong with young Jim Flynn? I saw you talkin' to him.

**Padraic**      The usual ... I think he's afraid ... more nervy than anythin' else. He'll be alright when the whistle is blown an' the ball is thrown in.

**Daigan**      I hope so. I hate fellows that have to work up their courage.

**Voice**      Padraic! Daigan! Are you coming?

**Daigan**      Come on, or we'll miss the boat.

*(They move away.)*

**Padraic**      Weren't you ever afraid yourself?

| | |
|---|---|
| **Daigan** | As big a coward as the next fellow, but that's not what I mean. Sure, there's nothin' to be afraid of in this world. I was only afraid of three things in my life. |
| **Padraic** | What? |
| **Daigan** | Rusty blades, casky porter an' parish priests' housekeepers.... Come on! |

# Curtain
*for end of Act I, Scene 1*

# Scene 2

*Action takes place in the kitchen of the house of Morisheen Brick in the village of Bealabawn in North Kerry. The time is near midnight of the day in question. Nellie Brick (Morisheen's daughter), a plain looking girl of 30, is sitting near the fire, darning socks. Near her is her young sister Bríd, a pretty girl, who is reading a woman's magazine.*

| | |
|---|---|
| **Bríd** | God! I'm jaded out! |
| **Nellie** | From doin' nothin'! Have you any notion o' goin' home? You're here a week now. |
| **Bríd** | I'll go when he comes for me. |
| **Nellie** | An' supposin' he don't come, what'll you do? Stay here with us for ever? If I know anythin', that's no way to treat a husband. |
| **Bríd** | If you know anything—that's just it! You don't know nothing! Sure, you were never with a man in your life! |
| **Nellie** | That's true! |
| **Bríd** | Sorry, Nellie! I didn't mean that. |
| **Nellie** | It's true, but it doesn't matter. Forget it! … There's our father…. |
| | *(Enter a bluff man with a crafty eye, of indeterminate age, in fisherman's garb. He carries a five-gallon container or bucket in his hand, staggers under the weight and is glad to leave it down.)* |
| **Morisheen** | Get up! Get up o' them chairs! We'll be havin' visitors in a few minutes. |
| **Bríd** | Visitors! |

| | |
|---|---|
| **Morisheen** | Footballers. |
| **Bríd** | Footballers! |
| **Morisheen** | The last footballer who stayed here was the mighty Elbows Magennis from Miltown Malbay. He had an elbow like a jackhammer. He blackened more eyes and more noses than Jack Johnson. A nice fellow. |
| **Bríd** | Footballers this hour of the night! Are you mad? |
| **Morisheen** | Why aren't you in bed? |
| **Nellie** | Leave her alone. She's a married woman, father. |
| **Morisheen** | Sorry Nellie! *(To Bríd)* Go up there to the room an' get ready the spare bed! |
| **Bríd** | You're not givin' me any orders! |
| **Morisheen** | God Almighty! 'Tis no wonder your husband is addled from you. I swear on my oath I'll leather the daylights out o' you if you don't do as you're told! |
| **Bríd** | I'm not goin' to be a skivvy for your drunken friends! |
| **Morisheen** | What's that? ... Go on, I'll...! |
| | *(Bríd does his bidding and exits.)* |
| **Morisheen** | She'd better modify or she'll be short a husband. |
| **Nellie** | The world will change her. |
| **Morisheen** | 'Tis the devil to see her married an' you scorned ... not scorned, Nellie ... I didn't mean that! |
| **Nellie** | Why are ye all so careful not to hurt my feelin's? I wouldn't care if I never married. You should know that by now Dad. |

| | |
|---|---|
| **Morisheen** | I know, Nellie, but if I had the way of it, 'tisn't a man I'd pick at all for you but a prince. |
| **Nellie** | *(Pushes him away affectionately)* Oh, you ould clown, you! |
| **Morisheen** | Cripes! An' he'd surely make a knight outa me. Sir Morisheen Brick, Bart. 'Tisn't but I've royal blood in my veins as it is, better than any Sugarin' Bart-in-et, from your great-great-great-great-great-great-grandmother. |
| **Nellie** | Go on, with you! |
| **Morisheen** | Oh, that's a gospel fact! There she was, back at the time of the Armada, a hand-some slip of a girl, with skin as smooth as an apple and black hair shiny like fresh tar, snug inside her bed when a tap comes to the window. 'Who's that?' says she. 'Open the window', says the voice. ''Tis me, the youngest son o' the King o' Spain, an' my ship is sank, my little Irish Senorita!' 'Come in here out o' the cold,' says she, 'an' I'll warm you!' |
| **Nellie** | You'll have me believin' you soon! Now, what was this you were sayin' about visit-ors? |
| **Morisheen** | There's a brown flood in the Shannon: heavy rain today in the Midlands, an' freshwater wholesale after comin' in to it. There's a boatload o' Clare footballers high an' dry. I invited two of 'em down for the night. They'll be off with the first light o' day. |
| **Nellie** | Oh, the Cuas lads! What about the rest of 'em? |

**Morisheen**    Gone off with women, or quartered in other houses.... They can be scourin' haysheds lookin' for 'em in the mornin'. You know the way them young hoboes scorn the bed and squeeze the last drop out of every hour of the night.

**Nellie**    An' are these two ould lads you're bringing here, or what?

**Morisheen**    Japers, no! One of 'em is Daigan the trainer, but the other fella is Padraic O'Dea, as fine a footballer as ever fielded a ball. You should see this man! Every bone well set in him an' a pair o' shoulders that would crack a stone wall for you. He's a quietly-spoken fella, too.... Like you, somewhat ... I'll bet anythin' he takes to you!

**Nellie**    Oh, for God's sake!

**Morisheen**    I'm serious! He's a fella that's advancin' well into years himself. You won't get a chance again.... By jingoes! If 'twas me I'd stop at nothin'. When I heard he was without a bed, I says to myself, that's the man for Nellie. Make the most o' your chances!

**Nellie**    What are you tryin' to say?

**Morisheen**    Nothin'...! Nothin' ... but it won't harm you to be polite to him.

**Nellie**    I'm always polite to people.

**Morisheen**    I know! ... I know! ... But 'tis like spoilin' a child ... wouldn't you put an extra bit o' jam on his bread if you wanted him to be fond o' you?

**Nellie**    Yes ... but how fond do you want me to be?

**Morisheen**    Ah, now you're making a mock o' me! ... Will that one below be able to tidy the bed alright?

**Nellie**    Ah, now Dad, give her half a chance!

**Morisheen**    Who's housekeeping for her husband, or does she expect him to hold a job and cook for himself as well?

**Nellie**    Ah, there's a neighbour o' theirs, a girl, that's keeping an eye to him.

**Morisheen**    Keepin' an eye to him, my tail! Good God, does she know anything about the world? Probably tryin' to get off with him ... when the cat is out!

**Nellie**    I suppose the pair that's coming will want something to eat. Is it a fry I'll put down for them or would they like somethin' cold? There's a fair share o' bacon left after the dinner.

**Morisheen**    Well, now, I asked them the same thing, an' they showed no interest at all in diet. Daigan the trainer it was that stuck a five-pound note into my hand and told me to order five gallons o' porter. Now, Daigan is a man who can be frightful pote-e-otic when he likes. 'When we're eatin', we're eatin',' says he, 'an' when we're drinkin', we're drinkin'!' ... I let it go at that.

**Nellie**    You would!

**Morisheen**    Isn't there enough arguin' in the world? Did you want me to start contradictin' them, an' they our guests for the night?

*(There is a knock at the door.)*

Them are they now! There's a great name

out o' these men for football. Show 'em res-
pects, Nellie, because there's a lot thought
of 'em at the other side o' the Shannon.

*(He opens the door. Enter Daigan followed by
Padraic who wears a light mackintosh over
togs and jersey. He has a handkerchief tied
about his head to ward off the rain, and he
carries a bundle of clothes in his hands.)*

**Morisheen**  *(Shakes their hands)* Welcome! ... This is my
daughter, Nellie ... she's single ... Nellie,
this is Daigan out o' Clare, an' Padraic
O'Dea, the footballer ... he's single, too.

*(Nellie shakes hands with both.)*

**Nellie**  The two of ye are drenched wet. Shove up
to the fire.

**Daigan**  Did you bring the porter?

**Morisheen**  'Tis there, an' here's your change. But,
lookit...! Ye'll have a tint o' this first.
'Twould bring you back from the dead!

*(He locates bottle of poitín in meal bin.)*

**Daigan**  Good God! Are ye makin' that here now?

**Morisheen**  We only makes barely enough for the cur-
in' of our own colds and cramps ... egg-
stands, Nellie!

**Daigan**  You used to play one time ... 'tis the walk
o' you I remember.

**Morisheen**  I played down on you. I sold you six dum-
mies, but I suppose you wouldn't remem-
ber that. Ye bate us the same day.... Ah! it's
a long time ago. That's the only time Bealabawn was ever beaten by Cuas.

**Daigan**  That's over thirty years ago! I was at a

wake the night before that game and I was still staggering as I stumbled out onto that field.

**Morisheen**     Right! An' ye could have won today, too! A bit o' luck an' ye had it.

**Daigan**        Maybe!

**Padraic**       Go on! Blame me if you want to. I know what they're all sayin'! One bad game, an' all the good games are forgotten.

**Daigan**        There's no one blaming you. You should have been playin' full forward, that's all! You hadn't the pace for midfield.

                  *(Nellie hands each a cup. Morisheen pours from the bottle.)*

**Padraic**       *(Explanatory to Morisheen)* I have football to burn, and I got the chances today, but when I went about changin' gears there was no power in my knees. 'Tis a sad thing, man, to have the heart an' the temper an' to find the limbs failin' you at the crucial moment.

**Morisheen**     I know what 'tis like, man! We all went through it. Didn't we, Daigan? ... Good luck!

                  *(They toast each other and sup from their cups. The Claremen are visibly affected by the drink.)*

**Daigan**        That wasn't made in a doctor's shop.

**Morisheen**     You're right it wasn't!

                  *(They each dip their cups into the porter gallon and swallow hastily.)*

| | |
|---|---|
| **Morisheen** | *(To Daigan)* Come on an' I'll get you out o' that wet trousers. Come on up to my quarters and I'll give you a dry pair.... |
| | *(Taking their cups of porter with them Morisheen and Daigan depart by exit taken by Bríd. Bríd immediately enters.)* |
| **Bríd** | Who's that? |
| **Nellie** | This is Padraic O'Dea out o' Clare. This is my sister, Bríd. She's married. |
| **Padraic** | Soft weather! |
| | *(They briefly shake hands.)* |
| **Bríd** | Who's the lad gone up into the room with my father? |
| **Padraic** | That's Daigan. He trains us. |
| **Bríd** | He didn't even salute me! Such ignorance! Are they all like that in Clare? |
| **Padraic** | No! There's ones like you there, too! |
| **Bríd** | Very smart, aren't you? He's a right lookin' thick, then, your trainer! |
| **Padraic** | That's a brainy man, Missie. |
| **Bríd** | *(Heading in direction of her own quarters)* I don't care if he had the brains o' Paul Singer, he has the head of an eejit! *(Exits.)* |
| **Padraic** | Fairly quick with the tongue, that one! |
| **Nellie** | I know where she got that. She's married to a man from Listowel, an' you know the kind o' tongues they have there. Listen— give me that bundle of clothes and I'll set 'em out to dry in front o' the fire. |
| | *(He hands her the bundle, which she unravels quickly.)* |

**Padraic**          Are we trouble to you? We could have just as easy gone to a hayshed.

**Nellie**           *(Laying clothes over chairs)* No trouble ... there's a spare bed, an' sure, Daigan is a bit o' company for my father. They'll be goin' back now over the games that were played forty years ago.

**Padraic**          Do you follow the football yourself?

**Nellie**           I saw you playin' a few times. I often saw you better than you were today.

**Padraic**          Ah! So you spotted it, too. I'm goin' off a bit now. I shouldn't have been playin' out the field, anyway.

**Nellie**           That's what they all said.

**Padraic**          Who?

**Nellie**           Oh, the crowd lookin' on. They said if you were playin' inside in the forwards, you'd have scored a few goals.

**Padraic**          'Tis aisy talk when the match is over.

**Nellie**           D'you want a mug o' porter?

**Padraic**          Aye, thanks!

                     *(Nellie fills cup and hands it to him.)*

**Nellie**           'Tis a wonder you didn't go to the dance like the rest of 'em or take up with some girl. I seen plenty of 'em there today.

**Padraic**          Ah 'sh, I never bothered my head about dancin', an' to tell you the truth I never courted a girl. Would you believe that—me thirty-five years and I don't know the taste of a girl's lips?

| | |
|---|---|
| **Nellie** | What? Have ye no girls back in Clare, then? |
| **Padraic** | Plenty! |
| **Nellie** | And how come you don't care? |
| **Padraic** | It isn't that I don't care. I never remember a woman in our house. My mother died when I was a baby, my father died a year later, broken heart. I had no sisters, no aunts. Football was my brother and sister, my father and mother. I loved football. I lived for it ... I'd die for football ... once. Fielding a ball from a cluster of hands, talons, you might say, possessing it then, owning it, playing with it, nursing it till an opening came. |
| **Nellie** | And the man in the room beyond, Daigan? |
| **Padraic** | My uncle. He reared me, taught me all I know. |
| **Nellie** | But not about girls! |
| **Padraic** | No, no girls. Football only, no time for girls. |
| **Nellie** | Don't you have a woman to clean up, to tidy? |
| **Padraic** | He's housekeeper too, my uncle. He does all, we get on fine. |
| **Nellie** | Take the coat off you an' heat your body to the fire. |
| | *(He takes off his coat and hands it to her. He wears togs and jersey.)* |
| **Nellie** | Is that some class of a new hat they have in Clare? |
| | *(Shamefacedly, he takes handkerchief from his head.)* |

| | |
|---|---|
| **Nellie** | Sit down ... I'll have the kettle boilin' in no time.... |
| **Padraic** | Tea is one thing I have no time for when I'm drinkin' an' Daigan is the same. One drink at a time, I say. |
| **Nellie** | Do you drink all the time then? |
| **Padraic** | Seldom enough! I drinks on Sundays and Holy days, fair days and patterns. I drinks then from morn till night and afterwards do be curin' myself for the rest o' the week. But no drink otherwise. 'Tis only to get out o' myself now an' again. |
| **Nellie** | What do you do for a living? |
| **Padraic** | Fisherman. |
| **Nellie** | What kind of a season are ye having? |
| **Padraic** | Not bad, not good! |
| **Nellie** | 'Tis bad enough to the West, by all accounts. |
| **Padraic** | Ah, there's a lot o' luck in fishin'! |
| **Nellie** | There's a scar in your hand. Did you come by that today? |
| **Padraic** | 'Tis nothin'! |
| **Nellie** | 'Tis nothin' now, but it could be a quare handful tomorrow. *(Takes his hand and examines it.)* You're right. 'Tis nothin' but a scratch. You have strong hands! |
| **Padraic** | Your arms are white. |
| **Nellie** | What are you lookin' at? |
| **Padraic** | Goose pimples. |

| | |
|---|---|
| **Nellie** | What about them? |
| **Padraic** | Nothin'! Only if there's one thing I like about women 'tis goose pimples. 'Tis the little way they set off the skin. |
| **Nellie** | Some people think 'em common. |
| **Padraic** | There's nothin' like goose pimples. I never touched a goose pimple. *(Gently, barely touches her arm)* 'Tis the cold that drives 'em out, isn't it? |
| **Nellie** | That's what they say. |
| **Padraic** | That's what I thought. |
| **Nellie** | An' I thought you told me you usen't to bother with women! |
| **Padraic** | *(Leaving her hand go)* I know! I know! But I amn't blind either. |
| **Nellie** | What used you be doin' when you should be chasin' women? |
| **Padraic** | I don't know! Give us another cup o' porter an' I'll give you the full history o' my life. |
| | *(Nellie takes his cup and fills it. Enter Morisheen with two cups. As he enters he is shouting back to Daigan who does not appear.)* |
| **Morisheen** | *(Ignoring the couple)* An' there was another fella with a baldy head from Lisdoonvarna. He attacked the sergeant of the Guards in Carrigaholt one night an' broke two plate-glass windows before they rounded him up. |
| **Daigan** | *(Unseen)* Casey. |
| **Morisheen** | Who? |

| | |
|---|---|
| **Daigan** | Thady Casey! A great man to field a greasy ball. |
| **Morisheen** | Hard thing to do! |
| | *(Morisheen fills both cups from the gallon.)* |
| **Morisheen** | *(To Nellie and Padraic)* Harder catch a comet than a greasy ball. *(Exiting carefully with full cups, stops and turns.)* Easier catch a mackerel than a greasy ball, easier catch a mermaid.... |
| **Nellie** | *(To Padraic)* You were goin' to tell me about the time when you should be courtin'. |
| **Padraic** | Oh, courtin'! I've it half-forgot now, what I used to be doin'. There was a crowd of us half-wild around Cuas an' we used go gallivantin' like stray cats till cockcrow. We used take the gates offa their hinges an' hang 'em offa trees an' put common cars up on the roofs o' houses, or if the night was fine, peel off our clothes an' go tumblin' like cock-salmon in the salt-water ... an' if there was meadows convenient we'd go gallopin' over them in our pelts an' be rollin' like donkeys in the young grass, or maybe go coursin' for ten miles along the coast o' Clare till the wind gave out on us an' we were fit for nothin' but the bed. I suppose you'll say we were half-cracked? |
| **Nellie** | Gor! Ye were full cracked! |
| **Padraic** | That's gone now. That's for younger men and boys. |
| **Nellie** | You're still a young man. |
| **Padraic** | Time to think of hanging up my boots. My pace is ... vanished ... pace don't come back. |

| | |
|---|---|
| **Nellie** | You don't have to play midfielder. |
| **Padraic** | Once a midfielder, always a midfielder. I'd never be satisfied on the wing or in a corner. I need space. I need freedom. |
| **Nellie** | What will you do? |
| **Padraic** | I suppose you have a lot of fellows after you here in Bealabawn...? |

*(Enter Morisheen followed by Daigan.)*

| | |
|---|---|
| **Morisheen** | Gimme a *Ciotóg* for the penalty. A good *Ciotóg* would drive a ball through a stone wall. |
| **Daigan** | 'Tis time for bed, I'm thinkin'. |
| **Nellie** | It's ready for you down there. |
| **Morisheen** | Yerra, what's your hurry man? Sure we'll have a talk first. There's a pile o' people in Clare I want to be enquirin' about. What about that fella with the buck teeth that used to stand in goals for Kilkee? |
| **Daigan** | *(Abruptly)* Are you for the bed, Padraic or not? |
| **Padraic** | Go to bed, let you ... I'll stay here till the porter is finished. |
| **Daigan** | You'll get stiff sittin' there like that ... you'll be cramped. |
| **Padraic** | Ah, you know, don't you, that I can't sleep in a bed with anyone. I'd only be kickin' like a jennet an' turnin' an' twistin' all night. |
| **Daigan** | Take the bed so, let you, an I'll sleep there in the settle. |
| **Padraic** | No! I'm staying here till the porter is drank. |

| | |
|---|---|
| **Daigan** | Have sense man, an' take your sleep! Don't you want to be picked for Munster? |
| **Padraic** | I'll be sleepin' for the rest o' the week. You take your sleep. |
| **Daigan** | *(Imperatively, so that Nellie and Morisheen start)* Get up to that bed and stop that nonsense! |
| **Padraic** | *(Coldly)* Aisy, Daigan, aisy! I'm thinkin', an' I'm in a mood for deep thinkin'. There's a lot in my mind. |
| **Daigan** | *(To Nellie)* Go to bed, let you! You'll only be keepin' him awake if you stay talkin' to him. |
| **Morisheen** | *(To Nellie)* Take your time! |
| **Daigan** | Can't ye let him alone, the two of ye? Do ye want to wear the man out? |
| **Morisheen** | We're doin' nothin' to him! 'Tis you that's doin' all the talkin'. By Jacos! You'd swear he was a child in swaddlin' clothes, the way you're talkin' to him. |
| **Daigan** | I'll talk to him whatever way I want! |
| **Padraic** | Go to bed, Daigan! |
| **Daigan** | I will, but let them go first. |
| **Morisheen** | *(After a pause)* Alright! But you're takin' great liberties in my house. It's a good job you were a footballer.... Good night, Padraic! |
| **Padraic** | Good night! ... Thanks for the shelter. |
| | *(Exit Nellie; and Morisheen after a hard look at Daigan.)* |
| **Daigan** | What was that one sayin' to you? |

| | |
|---|---|
| **Padraic** | Nothin' at all. We were just passin' the time. |
| **Daigan** | What did you say to her? |
| **Padraic** | Look, man, you'll have to stop this! I can't be accountin' for every word I say. |
| **Daigan** | Alright! Alright! But don't take any notice o' these people. Nothin' would suit your man better than to see you latchin' on to the daughter. She'll be firin' herself at you. Women are no good, man! |
| **Padraic** | Women are a sport I never took up, Daigan. But I'm gettin' a great notion for it, lately. I could hold my own at any game if I was shown how to play it, and if there was goals to be scored at it, I'd raise as many flags as any fellow, but there's no instructors for the game of women. |
| **Daigan** | What's gettin' into you at all? |
| **Padraic** | *(Angrily)* In the name o' God, leave me alone! Here I am, over thirty-five years of age and I hardly spoke ten words to a girl in my life. |
| **Daigan** | Aren't we happy enough, man? We were never short of anything. |
| **Padraic** | You might be happy, but I amn't! There I was, as contented as could be, talkin' to that girl and you come on and break it up! |
| **Daigan** | That one! |
| **Padraic** | Yes, that one! What's wrong with her? I know she's not a ravin' beauty, but she's nice and she's a fair girl to talk to an' I do be lonely sometimes, Daigan, for the company of a girl. I'd tell this to no one but you. |

| | |
|---|---|
| **Daigan** | *(Touched)* I'm sorry Padraic. I was only thinkin' of you ... I'm sorry ... wait till after you're selected for Munster, you can have the pick of 'em. |
| **Padraic** | I'll never be picked for Munster, not now. Didn't you see me today? |
| **Daigan** | One game only ... 'tis early in the season ... you'll be picked all right. This is your year. I know it, man. I feel it. I'll tell you the truth, though, I don't see what you want botherin' with women for. We have a contented house an' 'tis better to leave well alone. Is there some girl back in Cuas? |
| **Padraic** | There is not! There's a girl in my mind, though, a quiet, gentle girl that often kept me awake at night. |
| **Daigan** | Who is she? |
| **Padraic** | *(Annoyed)* Ah, she's no one! *(Tips his forehead.)* She's in here, man. That's what makes it tormentin'. I can't feel her or touch her. She's like a summer wind on the Shannon, fresh and clean and beautiful. I'd love to be stroking her hair in the moonlight maybe, down by the tide or to sit down with her somewhere quiet and study her face. What the hell do you know, Daigan? You never dreamed! |
| **Daigan** | Didn't I? |
| **Padraic** | Go on away to bed. I'm happy here. |
| **Daigan** | Be sensible, man, and take your night's sleep. |
| **Padraic** | *(Angrily)* I told you once, I told you twice, now I'm tellin' you for the third time ... |

|           | I'm stayin' here. Go on away to bed now. I've a lot o' weight on my mind. |
|-----------|---|
| Daigan    | If you change your mind, you can have the bed. |
| Padraic   | Alright! Only let me be! |
| Daigan    | Change into your clothes. |
| Padraic   | Alright! Alright! |
| Daigan    | Good night! |
| Padraic   | Good night! |

*(Exit Daigan. Padraic gets himself another cupful of stout and begins to unlace his football boots. As he does so he begins to sing the song 'The Hills of County Clare'. Enter Bríd.)*

| Bríd    | I don't suppose you heard anyone prowlin' around outside? |
|---------|---|
| Padraic | No ... not a sound.... Were you expectin' someone? |
| Bríd    | Don't be funny! |
| Padraic | I wasn't tryin' to be. |
| Bríd    | Well, I'm just tellin' you in case you do. |
| Padraic | You think he'll come, don't you? |
| Bríd    | *(Guiltily)* Who? |
| Padraic | Your husband. |
| Bríd    | What business is it of yours, I'd like to know? |
| Padraic | No business o' mine, except.... |
| Bríd    | Except what? |
| Padraic | Except you'll have to bend your head a bit |

with the breeze if you want to get on with people.

**Bríd**      I don't care if I never got on with people.

**Padraic**   Signs by, you can't pull with your husband. That's your trouble.

**Bríd**      Yes, it is my trouble, not yours. What do you know about trouble? You're not married.

**Padraic**   I have troubles in my head, girl, and all the combs in the world wouldn't get 'em out of it.

**Bríd**      Listen ... will you do me a favour?

**Padraic**   If I can!

**Bríd**      You'll be here, won't you, till daybreak?

**Padraic**   Yes.

**Bríd**      If you hear him around the house, will you go out to him?

**Padraic**   Why won't he come in?

**Bríd**      He's too proud to knock.

**Padraic**   An' what do you want me to do?

**Bríd**      If you hear him is there any chance you'd go out an' capture him?

**Padraic**   Is he wild, or what?

**Bríd**      No.... No, but hold on to him until I come out. Let out a roar and I'll hear you. Well, will you do it?

**Padraic**   Right! ... I can only be killed once!

**Bríd**      Thanks!

**Padraic**   But why don't you go home?

| | |
|---|---|
| **Bríd** | No hope! |
| **Padraic** | He'll be glad to see you. |
| **Bríd** | I wouldn't give him the satisfaction, and how do I know...? Maybe he won't want me. |
| **Padraic** | He'll want you. Why wouldn't he? |
| **Bríd** | Talk! |
| **Padraic** | What kind o' talk? |
| **Bríd** | Oh, neighbours that would be whisperin' about you if you passed the time o' day with another man. |
| **Padraic** | Hell isn't hot enough for anyone that comes between people that are fond of each other. |
| **Bríd** | That's the truest word you ever spoke. We could work out fine if we were left at it. We have our fights, but sure, everyone has them. |
| **Padraic** | What was this fight over? |
| **Bríd** | A silly thing. |
| **Padraic** | A sure sign that you're stone mad about each other. |
| **Bríd** | It was in the evenin' an' he was after comin' in from work. I poured out his tea an' some of it spilled in the saucer. He hates tea spilled in the saucer. |
| **Padraic** | So do I! ... Go on. |
| **Bríd** | 'Watch out the way you're pourin' that tea!' says he. 'You're awful particular!' says I. Then one word borrowed another an' I packed my traps an' came here. |

**Padraic**  How long ago is that?

**Bríd**  A week.

**Padraic**  Time to be makin' it up.

**Bríd**  I'm lonely for him.

**Padraic**  Go to him! As soon as you rise tomorrow, get up on a bicycle an' go straight home. Walk in the door to him an' throw the two hands around him an' I bet 'twill be a long time before you get your wind back after the squeezin' he'll give you.

**Bríd**  Would you say that?

**Padraic**  I'll swear it to you on a stack o' bibles!

**Bríd**  You're sure!

**Padraic**  Certain!

**Bríd**  I'll chance it in the morning. I'll chance it. 'Twon't be my fault. I'm a terror with the tongue, amn't I? I can't help it. It breaks out in me like dancin' or singin' in someone else.

**Padraic**  Or football!

**Bríd**  I'll slip up to bed. Change into your clothes … and listen to me … I'm sorry your team were beaten today.

**Padraic**  We'll rise again.

**Bríd**  You look lonely there!

**Padraic**  I'm nearly always lonely.

**Bríd**  A man needs a woman in his life three times, they say.

**Padraic**  Three times?

**Bríd**          When he's a baby to rear him, when he's at
                  the peak of his power to give him love, and
                  when he's old to nurse him.

**Padraic**       No! No, you're wrong. I'm beginning to
                  think a man needs a woman all the time.


# Curtain
*for end of Act I Scene 2*

# Scene 3

*Action takes place as before. One hour later, Padraic is sitting by the fire with a cup of porter in his hand. He sings slowly to the air of the Cuas song.*

*Enter Morisheen, barefooted. He is coatless. He wears shirt and trousers.*

**Padraic**

(*Sings*) Where shall I find the one I love?
A lady quaint and fair
As gentle as the cooing dove
with flowing soft brown hair.
I love her
I love her
Her loveliness I long to trace
I love her
I love her
Although I've never seen her face.

When shall I see my treasure trove
This lady quaint and fair?
When shall I walk beside my love
All through the land of Clare?
I love her
I love her
Would that she could hear my lay
I love her
I love her
I long to hold her night and day.

**Morisheen**

I knew a fellow from Carrigaholt that used to sing like that. He was a tall musty-lookin' fellow with a gullet like a crocodile.

He'd swallow anything provided there was alcohol in it. Do you know many songs?

**Padraic**      Awisha, an odd one here and there, sit up to the fire.

**Morisheen**    (*Filling a cup of porter*) Did you ever hear this one: 'There's nothin' like mate, said Paddy from Clare'? And another line; 'We'll be eatin' reheaters' (*pronounced ray-haters*) says Paddy from Clare'? Did you ever ate ray-heaters? Leftover boiled spuds you'd place among hot coals till the skin turned black. Then make a hole with your finger and drive in a blureen of butter. Food for angels, boy!

**Padraic**      I often ate them at night with a feed o' herrin's. Good fodder for a hungry belly.

**Morisheen**    Nothin' better! (*Sits down.*) What kind of a fella would you take me for? Tell the truth now and take your time. (*Morisheen poses as though for a photograph.*)

**Padraic**      A bit of a rogue, I'd say!

**Morisheen**    Great! Great! You're not far wrong. That's awful good that is—a bit of a rogue!

**Padraic**      A likeable rogue, though, with a tooth for a drop o' the hot stuff an' maybe now you're a man that would be no bad hand with the women. In fact, I'd say women would be pure putty in your hands.

**Morisheen**    (*Delighted*) The Gospel truth! ... Go on...!

**Padraic**      I'd want to know you better, but I'd say one thing for sure....

**Morisheen**    What's that?

**Padraic**          You've more in your head than shows in your face.

**Morisheen**          I like that.

**Padraic**          You're a brainy man.

**Morisheen**          Yes, yes, but a brain without looks is like a pod without peas. Dear God, a brain without looks is like a barrel without porter. Would you say now that I'm a comely man, a presentable man? (*Preens himself.*) Steady yourself now, take proper stock. Don't spare me now, let me have the naked truth.

**Padraic**          Well, you're healthy an' you're fresh an' you've a gamey eye. All things allowed, I'd say you're not a bad-lookin' young fella.

**Morisheen**          What age would you say I am?

**Padraic**          I haven't a clue, but 'tis certain you'll never play for the Kerry minors.

**Morisheen**          Well, I'll tell you! I left sixty some time ago an' now I'm a next-door neighbour o' seventy. But here's my trouble ... I have a powerful notion o' gettin' married again. Keep that under your hat. I've a strong notion, too, that I'd like to have a son ... I never had a son ... two daughters ... Nellie's an angel, but 'tis a son I'd like to have. I've great stories inside in me an' the most marvellous conglomeration o' painted lies you ever heard in your life but what's the good when I've no young fella to be tellin' 'em to? I'd apprentice him to every denomination of roguery an' humour so that he'd take the knocks o' the world in his stride an' break his behind laughin' at the invoices of misfortune.

| | |
|---|---|
| **Padraic** | Yes ... but have you the mother o' the child picked out? |
| **Morisheen** | A noble an' a forthright question! Do you know Listowel well? |
| **Padraic** | I played a few matches there. |
| **Morisheen** | Do you know Cockatoo Lane at all there? It's only possessed of seven cottages, a duckhouse and two henhouses. |
| **Padraic** | I think I have it now. Is it the first lane on the left as you go into town? |
| **Morisheen** | The very place. Well, there's a one-storey house there with two cannisters o' purple geraniums in the window an' a coop for pigeons up on a pole in the back yard. |
| **Padraic** | I think I noticed it once or twice. |
| **Morisheen** | Well, she lives there with her brother. He's a postman, a famished ould perisher. 'Twould break his heart to give you a registered letter. She's a bit with the forty, but we have an understandin'. |
| **Padraic** | Have you spoken to her? |
| **Morisheen** | Not exactly, but I often gave her a wink an' she gave a wink back. If I got ten minutes alone with her an' told her the advantages o' bein' married to me, I'd be a certainty. |
| **Padraic** | What about her brother? |
| **Morisheen** | Won't he have his letters an' his parcels? What more does he want? An' look at all the Christmas cards he'll be deliverin' an' Goddamit, what's to stop him from pickin' up a wife himself on his rounds. Hasn't he recourse to women every day of his life |

and hasn't he a uniform. A lot of women collapse at the sight of a uniform with never a thought for the commodities concealed underneath?

**Padraic**     Are you sure she'll marry you?

**Morisheen**   As sure as I'm talkin' to you! If she says no at first I'll pester her with parcels o' plaice an' whitin' an' another great plan is to saunter up an' down the lane outside her house until such time as she'll tell you come in or call the Guards to tell you go away. Man, dear, perseverance is a deadly weapon as far as women are concerned. I knew a widow one time from Cork an' she swore she'd never look at another man in her life the day her husband was buried. A month after, she was married to a fellow that used sharpen knives. He called to her door every day for thirty days an' sharpened all her cutlery an' never charged her a brown penny.

**Padraic**     Perseverance pays! You're sound in wind and limb?

**Morisheen**   Oh yes. Sound as a bell. A good man too around a house and a great man entirely in a bedroom. More porter?

**Padraic**     You took the words out o' my mouth.

**Morisheen**   (*As he fills cups*) D'you know what I heard an' ould schoolmaster o' mine say one time?

**Padraic**     Tell us!

**Morisheen**   He said porter in any shape or form is truly wonderful, and 'Maurice,' he said to me, 'the man that turns his back on porter for whiskey, turns his dial to the devil.'

**Padraic**     Did he now? I'd swear on my oath, your schoolmaster never said anythin' of the kind!

**Morisheen**   What does it matter what he said as long as some one said it?

**Padraic**     *(Accepting the cup of porter)* You're goin' gallant with the conversation but what made you get out o' the bed to come down to talk to me? I agree that there must be a certain amount o' roguery in the world. Now if 'tis roguery for a purpose, I'm all for it, but if 'tis needless roguery, you wouldn't blame a man for gettin' tired of it.

**Morisheen**   *(Sitting down and assuming a confidential pose)* You probably know what brought me down? You twigged it when you saw me comin'!

**Padraic**     I have a fair idea but of course a man can never be sure. State your case, anyway.

                *(They size each other up.)*

**Morisheen**   'Tis a delicate subject. I'm slow about it.

**Padraic**     'Tis about your daughter, isn't it?

**Morisheen**   Yes, 'tis about her. How did you guess?

**Padraic**     'Tis written all over you.

**Morisheen**   No more quibblin' so! Are you interested?

**Padraic**     No!

**Morisheen**   Are you positive?

**Padraic**     Well I hardly know her. I'm not condemnin' her, mind you.

**Morisheen**     The two of ye seemed to get on well enough.

**Padraic**       Seemed is right. We hadn't much time to like or dislike. I ... I just can't look over a woman like that and say yes or no.

**Morisheen**     You're not decided?

**Padraic**       Is she?

**Morisheen**     Well, to tell you the truth, I didn't say a word to her yet. I couldn't say it to her....

**Padraic**       And don't ... I'm not keen.... She's alright.... She's very nice and she's full o' courtesy, but she's not the kind of a girl I had in mind ... do you get my meaning? The way I had it in mind was to meet an honest, fair good-lookin' girl after a match some evenin' an' instead o' goin' drinkin' porter with Daigan, I'd inveigle her into goin' to the cinema an' maybe if we took to one another I'd propose to her an' we'd settle into the makin' o' children afterwards.

**Morisheen**     Ah! So that's the way!

**Padraic**       That's the way. Well like yourself I'd like to do my own pickin' and choosin'. I have certain notions and I want them fulfilled.

**Morisheen**     Things don't ever happen that way! No one ever gets the woman they dream about. Too much dreamin' about women spoils a man for other women. A woman in the flesh is worth ten in the mind. Nellie is here under your hands, alive and well. Your dreamy woman is neither here nor there.

| | |
|---|---|
| Padraic | True, true. But still a man would like to look around and find the nearest things to his dreams. |
| Morisheen | Do you know what's nice? Girls you'd see through the windows o' motorcars. They're here one minute an' gone the next. If you took them out o' the motorcars now they'd be just the same as ordinary girls as you'd see walkin' the streets. |
| Padraic | You miss nothin'! |
| Morisheen | I'll ask you once more ... are you interested in any way in Nellie? |
| Padraic | In no way whatsoever except to talk to her the same as any other human bein'. |

*(Enter Bríd with a small suitcase. She wears a coat and a headscarf.)*

| | |
|---|---|
| Morisheen | What's this? |
| Bríd | What's what? |
| Morisheen | What's the idea o' the bag, an' the coat on at this hour o' the night? |
| Bríd | I'm goin' back to Willie. |
| Morisheen | How, might I ask? |
| Bríd | On Nellie's bicycle, or do you expect me to walk? |
| Morisheen | An' who's goin' to collect it? |
| Bríd | You can collect it the next day you come to Listowel starin' at the postman's sister. You could do tricks up on it in front of her house like a schoolboy. |
| Morisheen | You're a flamin' rip! No wonder your husband don't put up with you. |

**Bríd**    (*Viciously*) An' whose fault is that, might I ask, but yours? 'Twas you rushed me into marriage the same way as you rushed Nellie into a convent so as you'd have the house here to yourself an' so's you could get married again.

**Morisheen**    If there weren't visitors in the house I'd turn you over my knee!

**Bríd**    Come near me an' I'll give you a welt o' this … (*Swings suitcase*) … you oul' gangster … you oul' pirate … no wonder you used be fillin' Willie with whiskey. Willie was fond enough o' me an' he'd have married me in due course if only you let well alone an' let things proceed naturally. But you couldn't wait. You rushed me into marriage when I was eighteen an' I havin' no qualification in the world for it, an' Willie worse again but we'll make out. I can thank this man from Clare because although he's the most ignorant man in the world with regard to women, he gave me a few honest answers. The next time you're inside with that oul' dexter from Cockatoo Lane, go down to the chemist's shop an' take a good dose o' Cascara. 'Twill do you more good in the long run.

    (*Exit Bríd.*)

**Padraic**    She's wise to go back to him.

**Morisheen**    I want no relation at all with a woman, only her company. You'd think I was a desperate ould dotard that did nothin' but chase women from the way she was talkin'.

**Padraic**    But don't you want a son?

| | |
|---|---|
| **Morisheen** | If an accident happens in marriage ... who're you goin' to put the blame on? |
| **Padraic** | You're a bigger rogue than I thought you were. |
| **Morisheen** | You still like me though! |
| **Padraic** | Yes, I like you! But you see my position in the other matter don't you? |
| **Morisheen** | I'll go back to bed now an' reconcile myself to loneliness for the rest o' my life. *(Exiting)* You could bring me great happiness if you changed your mind. |
| **Padraic** | You're expectin' too much of me. Man I'm nearly a black stranger to you. |
| **Morisheen** | I had a great song composed for the weddin' breakfast and I planned to spend the night of our honeymoon in Killarney. When I saw you today I said to myself there's a man that will save me from drownin' in loneliness. |
| **Padraic** | 'Tis tough! |
| **Morisheen** | There was a great prophecy related around here one time foretellin' wonderful events an' I thought when you came to the house tonight that you'd be part of it. I thought you were the man to bring the whole story true. |
| **Padraic** | I thought you were the biggest rogue in Bealabawn but now I'm thinkin' you're the biggest rogue in Ireland. What's the prophecy? |
| **Morisheen** | 'A man with a heart o' gold will swim the Shannon from Clare an' bring wonderful |

tidings to Kerry. A red-headed woman from Kilkee will give birth to a fiddler an' his music will convert Russia. An ass with an ear for music will be born in Banteer an' a man of seventy year will sire a noble son in the village of Bealabawn.'

## Curtain

*for end of Act I*

# ACT TWO

## Scene 1

*Action takes place as before. One hour later. Padraic sits, dressed, save for his small coat, which he holds across his knees. He would seem to be asleep. In the distance can he heard the melodeon playing 'God Save Ireland'. There are a few wild yells and whoops and the music grows louder and, suddenly there is a loud knocking at the door. Padraic stirs, rises, and goes to the door after repeated knocks.*

**Padraic**    Who's that?

**Voice**    'Tis me, Jim Flynn!

*(Padraic opens the door and admits him. Enter Jim Flynn, who we will remember from the first scene when the boat set out from Cuas.)*

**Jim**    We heard you were quartered here. Where's Daigan?

**Padraic**    He's asleep.

**Jim**    You missed a great night. You had a right to come with us. When the match was over, we took the banner—five or six of us —an' we followed a crowd o' girls as far as the town o' Listowel. We had a row there with a few o' the locals, an' we were arrested an' taken to the Barracks.

**Padraic**    What happened?

**Jim**    A couple o' size eleven boots in the rear end.

**Padraic**    They left ye go!

| | |
|---|---|
| Jim | Well, the sergeant said: 'Which would ye prefer, a night in the cells or a few rooters in the behind?' *(Rubs his behind.)* Them oul' Guards know how to give a kick in the pants.... Boy, let me tell you! |
| Padraic | What time will the water be ready? |
| Jim | About four hours, he said. 'Tis droppin' fast and there's a moderate tide in the morning. |
| Padraic | Sit down an' rest yourself. |
| Jim | Rest be damned! There's a crowd o' the local girls outside an' they know an oul' barn where we can have a bit of a dance. We have the music. Come on, man: we'll only be young once. |
| Padraic | I can't dance. Anyway there's the most of a gallon o' porter here an' I couldn't go without finishin' that.... |
| Elsie | *(Off)* Jimmy! Jim Flynn! |
| Jim | I'll be with you in a minute. |
| Padraic | I wouldn't want to go anyway. |
| Jim | We had hard luck today. Beaten by a bare point. I thought we had them there for a while. |
| Padraic | 'Twasn't your fault. You had a great game. There was nothin' to hold you. If we had a few more like you we'd have won well. |
| Jim | I never played better. What happened to you today? |
| Padraic | The same thing that'll happen to you some day. After a half an hour your bones will start creakin' like rusty hinges, *(Jim laughs)* |

an' you'll think there isn't enough air in the whole world to fill your lungs when the wind gives out on you. You're grand now. You're at your best. You're a cock o' the walk. For a few years you'll think that you're the strongest man that ever wore a jersey an' then suddenly one day you'll be running for a ball an' a young fella will pass you out an' you know 'tis time to hang up your boots. 'Tis sad, man, to be beaten by a fella that wouldn't hould a candle to you one time.

**Jim**            If I didn't know you, I'd say you were jealous o' me.

**Padraic**        Not jealous Jim, but I envy you because your best years are before you and mine are away behind. They're tied around my legs, holdin' me back.... The spirit is there alright. I'll never lose that and the jizz and the restlessness are inside of me but man, you can't fight the years and you can't match youth.

**Jim**            That's quare oul' talk! 'Tisn't like you!

**Padraic**        I'm changing, Jim. You mightn't understand it if I told you my heart was held back by my knees. Do you know what I'm going to tell you? I couldn't care less about football this night.

*(Enter a young girl, Elsie.)*

**Elsie**          Are you coming, Jim Flynn? The night is lightening and soon the dawn will be here and 'twill be too late for dancin'.

**Jim**            In a minute.

| | |
|---|---|
| **Elsie** | Come on! They're all gettin' impatient out-side. |
| | *(She goes to him and links his arm possess-ively.)* |
| **Padraic** | They used be after me too like that once but I never bothered with 'em. |
| **Elsie** | Who's he, Jimmy? Was he playing today? |
| **Jim** | *(Incredulously)* You're not tellin' me you don't know? Sure that's Padraic O'Dea. Everyone knows Padraic O'Dea. He was playin' centrefield today. |
| **Elsie** | Was he? |
| **Jim** | But surely you saw him today. |
| **Elsie** | If he was any good I'd have noticed him. Now come on away to the dance. My feet are itching to rise dust. |
| | *(There is the sound outside of the melodeon playing the same march, and the melodeon player enters, playing. He is followed by two men, one with football boots tied about his neck. They carry a banner between them which when unfolded reads: 'CUAS!' They are Pakey and Petey Mannon, Cooney is between them.)* |
| **Pakey** | *(Shrilly)* Up Cuas! |
| **Petey** | *(Rebelliously)* To hell with Bealabawn! |
| | *(Both yell and whoop loudly.)* |
| **Padraic** | In the honour o' God, pipe down or you'll wake what's in the house! |
| **Petey** | *(Noticing gallon, sniffs it.)* Jacos, Pakey, por-ter! |
| **Pakey** | Are you in earnest? |

| | |
|---|---|
| **Petey** | *(Gazing into gallon)* It has the black sudsy appearance o' porter. It has the strong stiff character o' porter an' it has the beautiful nourishin' smell o' porter *(flinging the banner aside he puts gallon to his mouth and swallows)*, an' it has the toppin' toothsome taste o' porter. |
| **Pakey** | Here, give me a cup out of it. I've a squadron of frogs' whelps in my windpipe from roarin' an' screechin'. *(He takes gallon and puts it to his head and swallows.)* Thank God for all things wet.... |
| **All** | Amen! Good luck and success to the Council of Trent who put fast on the meat but not on the drink! |
| **Pakey** | Padraic, you oul' devil, what are ye doin' here out o' the way? We've women outside an' a barn got for dancin' an' there's four hours before the boat leaves. |
| **Petey** | An' there's a stepdancer's moon in the sky. Come on away man an' dance the kinks out o' your muscles. |
| **Elsie** | Yerra leave him there if he don't want to come. He has the appearance of a fellow that would cut the toes off a girl. Who is he anyway? |
| **Pakey/Petey** | *(In total disbelief)* Who is he? Sure the world knows him. |
| | *(Enter Morisheen in a long nightshirt.)* |
| **Pakey** | Is it a man or a woman? |
| **Petey** | 'Tis neither. 'Tis a hoor's ghost. |
| **Morisheen** | What's all the commotion? |

| | |
|---|---|
| **Padraic** | There, now! I told ye that ye'd wake the house up. |
| **Morisheen** | Did they wake you, Padraic? |
| **Padraic** | I was only dozin' anyway. |
| **Morisheen** | *(To Pakey, Petey and Jim)* I saw ye playin' today. I wouldn't trust either one of ye with a penny balloon. |
| **Elsie** | *(Clinging to Jim)* An' here's the best footballer in Clare. |

*(There is a shocked silence while they all look at Padraic.)*

Well he is, an' he proved it today! Come on Jim boy, they're all mad jealous of you.

| | |
|---|---|
| **Morisheen** | You're Elsie MacDonagh, aren't you? |
| **Elsie** | That's right I am! |
| **Morisheen** | You should be in bed this hour o' the mornin'! When your mother was your age she was never out after ten. |
| **Elsie** | We're goin' dancin'. Will you come? You have a lovely outfit for it! |
| **Padraic** | Don't be disrespectful now to an old man. Shame for you and you under his roof! |
| **Morisheen** | Don't mind her, Padraic, you're wasting breath. |
| **Elsie** | You'd better be quiet, Clareman, or I'll give you a piece o' my mind too! |
| **Morisheen** | A piece of nothing is worth nothing. |
| **Elsie** | Very clever, aren't you, but as smart as you are the whole village knows your cuteness. *(To all)* He has two daughters. One of 'em |

|           | is always fightin' with her man an' the other one has no man to fight with. |
|-----------|--------|
| **Morisheen** | Shut up, you hussy! |
| **Elsie** | And what does he do? *(Indicates Padraic.)* He brings along your man here to know would he pawn the daughter over to him. A nice lob she'd have in you, an' you'd be in a nice way with her an' she in a convent for years but she couldn't stick that either, so she came away out of it. *(To Morisheen)* There now fox, that'll teach you to give lip to me! |
| **Morisheen** | You're a flamin' hussy! |
| **Padraic** | That's a terrible way to talk to a man in his own house. You show scant respect. What's the country comin' to? |
| **Morisheen** | You're right there Padraic. Good on you Boy! |
| **Elsie** | Are you goin' to let him talk to me like that, Jimmy? |
| **Jim** | You can't talk to her that way! |
| **Padraic** | Why not? |
| **Jim** | I say so. |
|           | *(Enter Daigan wearing his clothes but bare-footed)* |
| **Daigan** | What's this? |
| **Elsie** | Great God! What sort of a collection have you here at all? Is it a shop you have for repairin' ould crocks? |
| **Daigan** | Jim, get that rip out o' here! |
| **Elsie** | I'm no rip! |

| | |
|---|---|
| **Daigan** | Maybe not, but you're a forward young devil, whatever you are. |
| **Jim** | There's no one goin' to talk to her like that while I'm here. |
| **Daigan** | Do you know where you're talkin' young fellow? |
| **Pakey** | Come on away dancin', Jim! |
| **Petey** | That's right, Jim: we'll have a bit o' sport. |
| **Melodeon Player** | Come on, Jim, and don't spoil the night! |
| **Daigan** | If he wants to go in one piece, he'd better go now. |
| **Melodeon Player** | Come on Jim. |
| **Jim** | *(Pleading)* How can I go when I'm spoken to like that? |
| **Pakey** | Come on Jim. |
| **Petey** | You've a few drinks taken. |
| **Padraic** | Go on dancin', Jim, an' forget it! We'll all be friends back home in Cuas tomorrow an' you'll have that one forgotten. |
| **Jim** | Don't you tell me when to go. You weren't so hot today yourself. Only for me we'd be beaten twice the score. You left us down. |
| **Voice** | Take it aisy Jim. |
| **Jim** | You were supposed to be our star. You were advisin' me how to play this mornin' an' I listened to you an' I said to myself, 'Take note of that, Jim, let you because that's Padraic O'Dea talkin' an' he's a man that should be noted an' respected', but no—you flopped an' you flopped because |

you didn't try your heart out like you're always tellin' others to do.

**Petey**     That's not fair Jim.

**Voice**     Ah, will you take it aisy.

**Padraic**   What's gotten into you Jim? We used to be pals, you an' me. Is the matches we played an' the trainin' we did to be all forgotten in one bit of a night because a strange rip of a girl from North Kerry wants to see two men fightin' over her?

**Elsie**     Don't call me a rip!

**Jim**       Don't call her a rip...! *(Louder)* ... I said don't call her names. She's talkative an' all that, but she's a decent girl, so don't call her names.

**Padraic**   What's said is said. You know me. I don't backtrack.

**Jim**       Don't you? Well, you backtracked today and there'll be a new captain after the next meetin'. You can ask any o' the lads if you don't believe me.

**Padraic**   An' you'll be the next captain, I suppose....

**Jim**       Go on ... ask them.

**Padraic**   Is that right, Pakey...? Is it, Pakey?... well is it...? You, Petey, is that what the lads are sayin'? *(To melodeon player)* Frank, is this the talk ... is there to be a new captain? *(They are all noncommittal and somewhat hangdog.)* 'Tis the same in all jobs I suppose, when a man has his best given, he's kicked out an' pensioned off to make way for new blood—only there's no pension for footballers!

| | |
|---|---|
| **Jim** | 'Tis what the lads want! |
| **Elsie** | He's a better man than you! |
| **Padraic** | Is he? Are you Jim...? Are you a better man than me, Jim? It's no good sayin' it to yourself because the only one that'll believe it is yourself. If you want other people to believe it, you'll have to say it in public. Here's a chance to make a name for yourself! |
| **Daigan** | (*Coming and standing between them*) Have sense, lads! This bloody farce has gone far enough. Go on away to the dance, Jim. I take back what I said about your girl. We're all a bit irritated after today. Things didn't go right for any of us. |
| **Jim** | (*Pushing him aside*) Well, things didn't go badly for me today. Some said I was as good a man as ever came out o' Clare. |
| **Daigan** | If there was a way o' knowin' in the mornin' what way things would be in the evenin', we'd lock our doors an' come out from our kitchens no more! |
| **Jim** | Let that be the end o' your sermon now, Daigan. Padraic, for the last time, are you goin' to apologise to this girl? |
| **Padraic** | (*Calmly*) I can't apologise now, Jim, don't you see? It isn't the girl any more, or it isn't you or me. It seems to have grown up to be a big thing while we were talkin'. It's awful sad in a way. |
| **Jim** | (*Angry*) What are you talkin' about...? What's awful sad? |
| **Padraic** | I don't think you'd understand! ... I don't think there's anyone could understand. |

| | |
|---|---|
| Jim | Well, understand this, Padraic … *(menace)* … I'm puttin' it up to you … I'm askin' you to say you're sorry to this girl, an' if you don't, I'm askin' you to step outside an' I'll fight you to a finish. |
| Padraic | I don't want to fight you. Man dear, what good would that do either of us? |
| Jim | Well, say you're sorry so, an' we'll have done with it. |
| Padraic | She's the one that should be doin' the apologisin'! |
| Jim | *(Tensely)* Alright so … come on outside! |
| Padraic | No … what does it matter? I was a great footballer for years an' what does that mean now? If I fight you tonight, will it make me a better footballer and what will it mean tomorrow? |
| Jim | Are you funkin' me? |
| Padraic | I am! |
| Daigan | *(Shocked)* Padraic…! What are you sayin' man? Are you gone mad? |
| Padraic | I'm funkin' it … I'm not goin' to fight. He'd beat me anyway. A few years ago I'd have murdered him. Go away Jim an' find another young buck like yourself. You won't make much of a name for yourself out o' me. I was beaten today when my knees failed. |
| Jim | You're yellow! |
| Padraic | If that's the colour they give a man who doesn't want to fight, then I'm yellow. |

| | |
|---|---|
| **Jim** | You're a coward! |
| **Padraic** | Am I two things now? |
| **Jim** | I offered you fair fight an' you funked me. You're yellow! |
| **Pakey** | We saw one this evening in Listowel, an' she was blue! |
| **Elsie** | Shut up, you clown you! |
| **Pakey** | We did ...! We did! Ask Petey. |
| **Petey** | We did an' comin' out o' the barracks. |
| **Pakey** | 'Twas the sergeant's wife, she was trimmin' blossoms in the little garden in front o' the barracks. 'Are you foreign or a Mohammedan or what?' says Petey to her. 'What are you sayin'?' she said. ''Tis that blue head o' hair,' says Petey; 'we never saw the likes o' that in Cuas.' *(Nudges Elsie.)* An' d'you know what it was? 'Twas a blue rinse for four pence she bought in a shop.... |
| **Voices** | *(Offstage)* Come on out, if ye're comin' dancin'...! Come on an' bring the melodeon.... Ah, come on can't ye. We have a fiddler here from Lisselton and a drummer from Doon. |
| **Elsie** | Come on Jim.... You're the best man in Clare an' you proved it tonight. |
| **Morisheen** | Is it long since you looked in a mirror? |
| **Elsie** | Why?... Why? What's wrong? |
| **Morisheen** | Didn't anyone ever tell you that you have a jaw like a narrow black pudden, a pair of ears like the wings of a sidecar an' a nose like the yolk of a goose-egg an' as ignorant |

|           | an' as thick a skull you wouldn't find if you went rootin' through the graveyards of Ireland lookin' for specimens. |
| --- | --- |
| **Jim** | *(To Elsie)* Come on! Come on! He's only needlin' you. |
|           | *(Jim drags Elsie towards the door.)* |
| **Morisheen** | *(Shouting after them)* An' a poll on the crown o' your head like one o' them hairy baboons you'd see eatin' bananas in Duffy's Circus. |
| **Jim** | You funked it Padraic.... You funked me. 'Twill be the talk of Cuas tomorrow.... That I cowarded Padraic O'Dea. |
|           | *(Exit Jim and Elsie followed by Frank.)* |
| **Morisheen** | Anybody that knows Padraic O'Dea knows he isn't a coward. |
|           | *(Pakey and Petey begin to ready their banner for the exit.)* |
| **Pakey** | *(To Petey)* Is there any more left in the gallon? |
| **Morisheen** | *(Snatching the gallon)* If there is, 'twill go to the man that bought it. |
|           | *(Gallon in hand, Morisheen critically surveys Petey and Pakey. He walks around them, surveying them from head to toe. He pauses then, slightly to the side of them, staring at them intently.)* |
| **Pakey** | Why are you starin' at us? |
| **Petey** | Yes ... that's the lookin' he has at us! You'd think we were racehorses or somethin'! |
| **Morisheen** | Well racehorses is one thing an' donkeys is |

|  | another thing an' anyone can see that you aren't racehorses! |
|---|---|
| **Petey** | What's all the lookin' for? |
| **Morisheen** | *(Still surveying them critically)* 'Tis hard to tell … *(mock puzzlement)* … very hard to say which it is. |
| **Pakey** | Which is what? |
| **Petey** | What is which? |
| **Morisheen** | It has me puzzled since the two of ye walk-ed into the house. |
| **Pakey & Petey** | *(Retreating towards the door)* What? … What? |
| **Morisheen** | Which of the two of ye is the bigger eejit? |
| **Pakey** | *(Whoops first.)* Up Cuas! Glory, Cuas! |
| **Petey** | Down with Bealabawn! To hell with Beala-bawn! … Herrin'-chokers an' pratey-snappers…. |
|  | *(Then with a series of wild yells, they are gone, singing 'The Cuas Boys'.)* |
| **Morisheen** | They're not broken in at all yet … shouldn't be let out for a few more years…. Don't take any notice o' that girl. She's a thunderin' hussy since she went workin' to Listowel. Would you like to take my bed for a while, Padraic? |
| **Padraic** | No thanks! |
| **Daigan** | I never thought I'd live to see the day Padraic O'Dea was cowarded. Your name will be mud in Clare, to be cowarded by young Jim Flynn and he no more than a boy! I didn't think there was a man in the |

|           | globe could walk up to you an' call you yellow. |
|-----------|-------------------------------------------------|
| Padraic   | Not makin' you a short answer, he can call me whatever he likes. |
| Morisheen | Young cocks always crow the loudest. Why bother with him? |
| Daigan    | Of course he'd beat you. He's a faster man and he's at his best an' you aren't but that doesn't give you any call to back down. |
| Padraic   | That wasn't why I backed down. Look, Daigan, I'm after resolvin' somethin' to myself an' in a way I'm contented. I want to hear no more about it now or you'll find me losin' my temper. |
| Daigan    | The man you should have lost your temper with is gone out the door. If you want to lose it there's still time to follow him and put it up to him and fight until you're not able to stand up any more and that way you'll keep your good name and I'll be able to keep my head high when I go back to Cuas. |
| Padraic   | Go to blazes! |
| Daigan    | What? |
| Padraic   | That's what I said! Go to blazes an' stay there. You're only worried about yourself. It don't matter a hang one way or the other to me, man, what anyone thinks. I'll have tears o' my own to be sheddin' tomorra an' I can see no one puttin' their hand on my shoulder an' sayin' 'Cheer up Padraic, you were a prince among men one time'. |
| Daigan    | There's still time to go after Jim Flynn an' |

make him eat his words. You can beat him
if I let him have an odd one from behind.
I'll sidle in with a quick one when he isn't
looking.

Padraic

That's not my way o' fightin'. I'd never
stoop to that.

Daigan

(Contemptuous) Go away then with your
tail between your legs.

Padraic

Go to bed, Daigan, or by the Lord God that
made me, I'll crack your jaw! Don't pester
me like an oul' woman, or I'll go for you!

Daigan

I've given you up! I don't know what's
happened to you.

Padraic

Listen to me, Daigan. My football days are
over. My strength is left to me but my
timing is gone and my pace is squandered.
I was the finest athlete in Clare but now
I'm finished I'm just an ordinary fisher-
man. That's my lot. I'll never be shoulder-
ed off the field again. I'm lucky to have my
fishin'. I'll go out now an' I'll fight Flynn,
not for you Daigan, or not for my own
pride. I'll fight him because it was to be. I
want room for my boat when I pull into the
pier at Cuas an' room on the strand for my
nets to dry an' room on the fishin'-banks
for my haul—otherwise I'd be pushed out
an' that'd be the end o' me. (Rolls up his
sleeves, spits on his hands and flexes his fists.)
You taught me Daigan. Close up your fists
until you make weapons out o' them. Remember! Squeeze your fingers into a ball o'
bone an' put your shoulder behind every
clout so that when you hit a man his head
will ring an' he won't come lookin' for

more. *(Pitifully, then almost on the verge of tears)* Because don't you see, I'm a man out o' the village o' Cuas an' there's this jizz, this terrible bloody jizz inside o' me. I can't lie low like others and I can't cry my troubles out loud like a woman. I'd as lief be dead as be the way I am now.

*(Padraic goes slowly out the door. Daigan moves to follow but Morisheen gestures him to stay back and both men look after the retreating figure.)*

# Curtain
*for end of Act II, Scene 1*

# Scene 2

*Action takes place as before. Time—Daybreak. From barn down the road comes the sound of a sleepy waltz. Daigan enters.*

| | |
|---|---|
| **Daigan** | There's no sign o' Padraic, I suppose? |
| **Nellie** | No…! When I came down into the kitchen he was gone. Strange, isn't it, that he should go off like that? He didn't take his gear with him. |
| **Daigan** | He'll be back. |
| **Nellie** | Maybe he went down to the dance. |
| **Daigan** | No … no … not Padraic. |
| **Nellie** | Will you take a few eggs with your breakfast? |
| **Daigan** | No, I'll just take a cup of tea till Padraic comes…. D'you hear that music? Do they think that music is the only thing in the world? Music won't fill a hatch with herrings or open drills for potatoes. |
| **Nellie** | Aye, I heard them, they're at it all night long. |
| **Daigan** | It's a disgrace! Music, dancing, courting and roars out of them. Smoke-filled halls like dungeons … and women that couldn't boil an egg for you. |
| **Nellie** | They might as well enjoy themselves. Soon enough they'll have to face the world. Dancing is harmless. |
| **Daigan** | A couple o' more nights like last night an' |

my lads wouldn't beat a team of oul' women. The music is stopped. It couldn't last.
They started off with hornpipes and jigs
an' reels, then Sieges of Ennis, then quick-
steps an' waltzes an' now they're finishing
up with slow waltzes.

**Nellie**      Everythin' wears itself out.

**Daigan**     There are some things that don't.

**Nellie**      What for instance? All things last their
proper length.

**Daigan**     The sea! Ships get weary an' men get weary, footballers get weary. Even the rocks do
be worn away but the sea never gets weary. You couldn't tire the sea.... I wonder
what's happened to Padraic. The sea never
sleeps and you'll never see the sea without
life. Where the hell can he be? *(Rises.)*

**Nellie**      You sound worried!

**Daigan**     *(Nervously)* I'm not! ... I'm not! ... Why
should you go an' say that? What's there to
be worried about? ... I'm not worried.... I
was never worried about Padraic. You've
no right to say that.

**Nellie**      Sorry!

*(Enter Morisheen.)*

**Morisheen**   Ah! There you are Daigan.... Did you sleep
well?

**Daigan**     I only slept in patches. That bloody music
kept wakin' me up.

**Morisheen**   You forgot to say your prayers—that's
what happened!

**Daigan**     Must you be always so damn smart?

| | |
|---|---|
| **Morisheen** | I can't help it if you didn't sleep. What did you want me to do? Go up to the bed and sing 'Clare's Dragoons' till you dropped off? |
| **Daigan** | I'm always remindin' myself that no one should pay attention to a fool an' here I am, listenin' to you! |
| **Morisheen** | Where's Padraic? ... Isn't he back yet? |
| **Daigan** | I'll be goin' out now in a minute to see would I find him. |
| **Morisheen** | Why don't you leave him alone for a change? |
| **Daigan** | Mind your own business. |
| **Morisheen** | Let him alone! He's a grown man. You're breathin' down the back o' his neck for years. He can't go left or right without your approval. He has a life of his own to live, especially now. |
| **Daigan** | What are you talking about? |
| **Morisheen** | You want him to be all the things you never were. You failed at football yourself and you tried to turn Padraic into the greatest ball player of all time. You should know what the years do to footballers, Daigan, what they've done to Padraic. The years have outfielded him at last, outstripped him, left him stranded. |
| **Daigan** | He was a genius, I tell you, a genius. No one had his craft. |
| **Morisheen** | Aye! But geniuses are quare people. They're to be pitied when time takes it all away. They can't ever knock at the door and come in to the happy crowd and be |

part of it. No, they have to keep company with other things—things like the wind, and the rain and the sea—the most sorrowful things. Leave Padraic alone, man, in the honour of God an' he'll come around. But he must work it out for himself.

**Daigan**

(*Furious*) You schemin' connivin' oul' hypocrite! You're the one that had the biggest plan of all made for him. You thought you had nothin' to do but bring him here to the house, an' this one here, this ex-nun with the shiny face that you'd imagine butter wouldn't melt in her mouth. There's women in Clare would fall at his feet if he bothered to pass the time o' day with 'em, an' you fancyin' you were fit for him. Gor! 'tis the joke o' the year ... I could die with the laughin'!

**Nellie**

(*Hurt*) What started all this? I never saw him before last night. I don't care for him an' I don't want him.

**Daigan**

Don't you though! You'd stop at nothin' to get him. I saw it written all over you. You were well primed by that oul' villain over there. You knew you had an innocent boy with no knowledge at all of women. You'd draw the line at nothin' if you thought you could have him. A reject, that's what you are ... a bloody reject.... You couldn't stay with the nuns because you were gettin' restless, gettin' anxious for the world. You couldn't sleep nights so you left and you came home to Dad. But Dad didn't want you either. Dad had different plans entirely.

| | |
|---|---|
| **Morisheen** | For God's sake, stop it, man! |
| **Daigan** | *(Now in a frenzy)* What sort o' fools did you take us for? Did you think we passed up marriageable women in all the towns of Ireland to come here an' be fooled by a woman like you that will be old and grey in ten years? |
| **Morisheen** | Well, if she'll be old and grey in ten years, you'll be growing daisies in less. |
| **Nellie** | Stop it! Please, stop it! This is all wrong. This is a mistake. |
| **Daigan** | It's the truth, you bitch. Nothin' would suit you better than to chain my fine boy. |
| **Morisheen** | Your boy? He's not your boy! You don't own him. You're ruining him … your boy. |
| **Daigan** | I reared him an' trained him an' taught him all he knows. I spoon-fed him and washed him with those two hands since he was a child. I never let a woman near the house to wash or cook for us. I did it all myself. |
| **Morisheen** | An' for all you taught him does he know happiness? Does he know peace of mind? The poor fellow can't even think for himself. I know he'll never take Nellie but he wouldn't get a better woman if he searched till he dropped an' that's one thing I mean from my heart because I know Nellie and I know the kind of girl she is. |
| **Daigan** | An' so do I an' I'll tell her! You're not good-lookin'! You're not well-made an' you're backward. Your manner is dull an' your wits are slow an' deny it if you like. |

There might be a man for you somewhere but Padraic O'Dea isn't that man.

**Nellie**   *(Broken)* I'm not denyin' myself. You painted a true likeness o' me. There's no place for girls like me, is there? The like of me were born to mind other people's children or to sit in a corner out of the way. But what about the girls like me, the bashful girls, the dull girls, the withdrawn girls? Who's to write lovesongs for us? Is it because we don't present a fair picture on the outside that there's nothin' inside of us? What do you want me to do? Go away an' drown myself? There's a place for people like me too. God wouldn't have made ordinary girls and shy girls unless He had plans for us. It's because we are the way we are that nobody will ever know our great capacity for love.

**Morisheen**   You're too good for him, Nellie.

**Daigan**   *(Indicating Morisheen)* An' I suppose God has plans for him too? *(To Morisheen)* You couldn't give her away for nothin': if you gave a million pounds with her, you wouldn't get a dacent man to take her.

*(Nellie bends her head into her hands.)*

**Morisheen**   *(Infuriated, takes a knife from the dresser)* Here take that an' stick it through her! Go on man: why are you lookin' at it? Take it an' ram it into her an' finish off what you started…. Go on! … She won't feel it after the stabs you've given her already. Look at her bleedin' man! *(Shouting)* Look into her heart an' you'll see the blood floodin' out of it like an ebb tide … look into her eyes an' see the hurt that's in them ... no, you couldn't see ... not you—you're blinded by your own bitterness.

**Daigan**    (*Recoils confused.*) Padraic ... I've got to find Padraic.

*(Morisheen turns his attention to Nellie who is still bent over the table.)*

**Morisheen**    (*Disgusted*) You don't want to take any notice o' what that fellow said. The world is full o' bitter men like him. He's all twisted up for the want of a woman. Listen to me! Listen to me.... We'll be happy here, the two of us. We'll have each other for company. Nellie girl, don't take on like that.

*(Nellie raises her head and dries her eyes.)*

**Nellie**    What's for me Dad? What's to become o' me? I have nowhere to go.

**Morisheen**    You'll be alright, Nellie. I'll care for you.

**Nellie**    You will, an' are you goin' to live for ever?

**Morisheen**    You'll have Bríd. She'll be glad of you.

**Nellie**    And be a nursemaid to her children. When the children are grown up, where am I then? Who'll want me, Dad? I'll be alone.

**Morisheen**    I'll be here for years yet.

**Nellie**    No, you won't. It wouldn't be fair to you. I know all about that woman in Cockatoo Lane. You'll be pinin' for her all the time. Don't worry! You think I don't understand? I'll go housekeepin', that's what I'll do ... I'll go housekeepin' for a priest. I have to look out for myself ... I've let it go too long.

**Morisheen**    You'll go nowhere. You'll stay here with me.

**Nellie**    No ... that's what I'll do. My mind is made up. I'll housekeep for a priest in some quiet parish where I won't be known.

**Morisheen**    That's nonsense! I won't have that an' that's final ... I've been a quare father, haven't I, Nellie? Well I won't be so. You'll be happy here. You don't know the humour that's in me if I want to try. I'll have you in stitches from one end of the day to the other. Sure I'm too ould a buck to marry anyway. I'd collapse if I got a grueller in the first buckle. My eyes'd close and my knees'd buckle. Could you imagine me after a honeymoon with my body black and blue and my tongue hangin' out? I can see her comin' after me *(Protects himself)* lookin' for more, game to the tail with a glint in her eye and me a dead duck on the flat o' my back. I wouldn't last as long as a hailstone in a hot fryin' pan. Cripes, Nellie, if you see me making for matrimony will you notify the undertaker?

**Nellie**    It's no good, Dad. It's no good at all, I'd only be depressin' you. Don't you know what old maids are like in a house? And worse I'd be gettin' as I got older.

**Morisheen**    Not with me, you wouldn't. I was down the river last winter and I saw a long-legged crane trying to break the ice to get a drink. Up comes a sparra, 'Anything doin'?' sez he to the crane. 'No good', sez the crane. 'Ah,' sez the sparra, 'we didn't drink enough of it while we had it.'

*(From the distance discordant yells and shouts are heard—growing louder.)*

**Morisheen**  'Tis them two lunatics that were here last night!

*(Cries of 'Up Cuas!' and 'To hell with Beal-abawn!' Enter Pakey followed by Petey.)*

**Pakey**  Where's Daigan and Padraic?

**Petey**  Where's Padraic and Daigan?

**Morisheen**  They're not here.

**Petey**  The water is down in the Shannon an' the lad with the boat said he'd be chargin' double time from this on.

**Pakey**  Double time. Good God, that's twice the price! 'Tis daylight robbery.

**Morisheen**  And he should get danger money too!

**Pakey**  Why?

**Petey**  Why so?

**Morisheen**  For transporting a cargo of certified eejits like the two of you.

**Nellie**  Sit down and have a cup of tea before ye start.

**Pakey**  No, thanks. I'm after two huge cuts o' seed cake an ould woman gave me an' a fine saucepan o' new milk an' Petey here went home with a schoolmaster's daughter to a three-storey-high house an' they gave him bacon an' eggs an' what else was it, Petey?

**Petey**  Stuffed tomatoes an' them small knobs o' tender scones an' the schoolmaster invited me over for the pattern on the fifteenth of August.

| | |
|---|---|
| **Morisheen** | And do you know why he invited you? Did he explain it to you? |
| **Petey** | No. |
| **Morisheen** | He wasn't fair now when he never told you why he invited you. |
| **Petey** | Why so? |
| **Pakey** | Why so? |
| **Petey** | Why so did he invite me? |
| **Morisheen** | The place to be black with people that day an' make a fortune chargin' people to have a look at you. |
| **Pakey** | Come on away Petey. This oul' fellow is always coddin' us. |
| **Morisheen** | Go easy a minute. What way did the fight go last night? |
| **Pakey** | Padraic O'Dea got the razz. |
| **Petey** | He got it alright. Talk about shoein' a wheel.... He got at least forty flamin' licks into the kisser an' as many more on top o' the sconce. |
| **Pakey** | He got the stuffin' knocked out o' him in a fair fight. They were at it nearly half an hour but Jim Flynn was too quick for him. |
| **Petey** | 'Twas the first time I ever saw Padraic O'Dea capsized. |
| **Morisheen** | Where did he go after? |
| **Petey** | Don't you know the way fellas like that do be? We left him there grindin' his teeth an' cuttin' his tongue and cryin' to himself an' thinkin' of all the wrongs the world did |

him from the day he was born. That's the
way fellas like that do be.

**Pakey**        That's the way fellas like that do be alright.

**Morisheen**        Well, Padraic isn't here now but Daigan
went lookin' for him. We'll send them to
the boat as soon as they turn up. Don't go
without them. Are all the dancers gone
home?

**Pakey**        They're all gone. We left one fella from
Kilkee below doin' the Hokey Pokey.

**Nellie**        Have one mouthful o' tea.

**Pakey**        We haven't time. We're under orders from
the fella that owns the boat to round up all
the lads. We've them all contacted now
except Padraic and Daigan and Cooney the
corner forward.

**Morisheen**        Who's he?

**Pakey**        Yirra, Cooney, the corner forward. He was
in Listowel last night. He was to follow us
on. We couldn't be waitin' for him.

**Petey**        The last time I saw him he was sitting
down at a table with a blondie-haired one
from Listowel. Chips an' sausages he was
eatin' and the blondie one had a big plate
o' them sticky buns in front of her. 'Tis
nearly ten miles of a rough road to Listowel.

**Morisheen**        He won't feel it.... He'll have light pockets
after the blonde.

**Pakey**        We'll be off. That fellow's asleep in some
hayshed.

| | |
|---|---|
| **Petey** | Maybe stuck in a hole in a ditch, drowned or well colonised with common fleas under a rick. |
| **Nellie** | Listen … take a couple o' slices o' bacon with ye in case the hunger catches ye. |
| **Pakey** | Is it lean or fat or streaky? |
| **Morisheen** | Streaky. |
| | *(Nellie cuts a few slices of bacon.)* |
| **Petey** | Is it sweet? |
| **Morisheen** | As sweet as the breast of a Duhallow drake. |
| | *(Nellie hands them the bacon.)* |
| **Pakey** | God bless your hands! |
| | *(Immediately they stuff their mouths with bacon.)* |
| **Petey** | 'Tis nicely tasting. |
| **Pakey** | Up Cuas! |
| **Petey** | Up Cuas! *(They both yell and whoop.)* |
| **Pakey** | Down Bealabawn! |
| **Petey** | To hell with Bealabawn! |
| | *(Both yelling, exit.)* |
| **Morisheen** | Cracked as the crows! You can't whack the youth. |
| **Nellie** | I didn't know there was a fight last night. What started it? |
| **Morisheen** | They were crowning a new King. A young fellow called Flynn played well yesterday, and there was a girl here last night. 'Twas inevitable. |

**Nellie**         Did he get a bad beating?

**Morisheen**      I'm afraid so. You'd be a long while getting the better of a man like him.

**Nellie**         Maybe he's thrown down unconscious somewhere. Should we look for him?

**Morisheen**      Padraic is a man who will have to advance up to himself to be reckernised before he ruins himself. Sometimes a man needs to talk to himself. Best let him be.

*(Enter Daigan, alarmed.)*

**Daigan**         He didn't show?

**Morisheen**      No.

**Daigan**         An' where would he be gone? *(He goes to door and calls)* Padraic! ... *(Exiting, calls)* Padraic! ... Padraic! ... *(Exits distractedly.)*

*(Nellie pours a cup of tea.)*

**Morisheen**      Well 'twas a full night an' mornin'. What Daigan said meant nothin' at all. You're pleasant-lookin' an' easy to get along with. Sure a body would never know you'd be in the house, you're so quiet. You're clean and tidy and your feedin' is fit for the Pope o' Rome.

**Nellie**         You never give up tryin'! You won't have to be trying for long more for my sake.

*(A figure appears at the door—Padraic O'Dea. He is obviously at the end of his tether.)*

**Morisheen**      Padraic ... Padraic.... Good God, man, you're done in completely. Where were you?

*(Morisheen and Nellie rise hastily to assist him—they lead him to a chair. Nellie hurries to a cupboard and gets small bowl which she places on table.)*

**Nellie**     *(Searching drawer of cupboard)* Lint! ... Lint! ... Where's the Lint?

**Morisheen**     You're a sight, man!

**Nellie**     Ah, thank God, here it is.

*(Finds scissors cuts square—places it in bowl, fetches kettle and pours water into bowl. Morisheen is kneeling, feeling Padraic's face and cuts.)*

**Morisheen**     You took a frightful hammerin'!

**Padraic**     'Twasn't the beatin' so much. I've gone through my own Gethsemane this night.

**Morisheen**     Ah, I know! ... I know! ... God help us. I know well what 'twas like with you.

**Padraic**     Sorry to be such a nuisance! ... Where's Daigan?

**Morisheen**     He's gone searchin' for you ... the man is distracted worrying about you.

**Padraic**     If he found me like this I'd have choked him.

**Nellie**     You have great healin'. Your cuts are closed an' there's no infection.

**Padraic**     I dipped my head in a pool o' salt-water an' held it under till I nearly suffocated. I did that twenty times if I did it once because my head was openin' and splittin' with concussion. I don't know what got into me then because I stripped off my clothes an' went out into the sea up to my neck and I stood there and let the hands of the tide search me and I let the small waves wash over my body because I was sore and there was an ache in every part o' me.

**Morisheen**  You had a rough night, boy.

**Padraic**  I rose out o' the water then an' drew my clothes on me an' stole up to the side of the barn where the dancin' was an' I peeped in through a crack in the wall an' there they were inside dancin' an' singin' an' huggin' an' I might be dead for all they knew an' you'd swear that a man of my mettle never suffered a defeat that night because the crowd inside were conductin' themselves the same as if nothin' happened an' I said to myself, 'Does anyone want me or what is it that's in me that makes me stay outside the crowd an' be a black stranger to people I've known all my life?'

**Morisheen**  Every man is a stranger to his neighbour and the nearer the neighbour, the bigger the stranger. It's only an act, all this good-fellowship an' back-slappin' an' hand-shakin' an' praisin'. No one means it in earnest. It's the thing to do. A man must stand alone while he's findin' himself.

**Padraic**  I'll have to be goin'. The boat will be waitin' an' the water is fit for crossin'. *(He tries weakly to rise but they restrain him.)* I'm fagged out.

**Morisheen**  Go to bed for an hour or two an' I'll think o' some plan to delay the boat. You don't want to be seen in that state.

| | |
|---|---|
| **Padraic** | *(Swelling)* What do I care about them? What do I give a hang about any of them? |
| **Morisheen** | The spirit is in you all the time. You'll never lose that ... but you must get it into your head you lost the fight. |
| **Padraic** | I'm getting it into my head thro' all the sneaky entrances I know. |
| **Nellie** | Go to my bed for an hour. It's soft an' it's warm an' it's at the back o' the house where you'll not be disturbed. |
| **Padraic** | No ... thanks all the same.... If I went to sleep now I wouldn't wake for a month. I'll be alright. |
| **Nellie** | I'll get a cup o' tea for you. |
| **Morisheen** | An' I'll put a lacer o' the hot stuff in it. |
| **Padraic** | No hot stuff ... Sundays an' Holy Days only! ... I thought a lot of things an' I out there up to my neck in water. I can walk across now to Clare, I said to myself and before I'm gone a hundred feet my worries in this world'll be over. |
| **Morisheen** | A natural thought considerin' the circumstances. |

*(Nellie hands Padraic a cup of tea.)*

| | |
|---|---|
| **Padraic** | But a strange thing, I thought about you. |

*(Nellie turns away. Padraic looks into the distance.)*

| | |
|---|---|
| **Padraic** | I thought about the little talk we had last night and I said to myself, now don't laugh at me, that girl had pure eyes and eyes as clear as the green ice of winter where |

eagles fly.... Don't laugh at me for the love of God.

*(Morisheen slides discreetly towards room — Nellie stands with her back turned to Padraic —Padraic rises and addresses her.)*

**Padraic**

Don't laugh at me for the love o' God, whatever else, because that's one thing I couldn't stand.

**Nellie**

*(Without turning)* I won't laugh at you. That's one thing you can be sure of. But that's all I'll promise you because you'll be goin' away for good to Clare in a short while and you'll have forgotten whatever you're likely to say by tomorrow.

**Padraic**

That's where you're wrong, if you knew me you'd know I was never a man for idle talk. I say what I mean and I never say anythin' easily an' maybe that's my trouble. That's the kind o' man I am.

*(Enter Daigan.)*

**Daigan**

Thank God! ... Thank God! ... You're fine ... you're grand. I didn't know what happened to you. 'Tis great to see you. 'Tis new life to me to see you. New life, man.

*(Padraic is not even aware of his existence.)*

Look Padraic ... look ... you stay here as long as you want an' I'll go down an' hold the boat ... don't be in a hurry, they won't go without you ... an' lookit, if you're goin' to be talkin' to that girl tell her that I'm sorry deep down in the bottom of my heart for hurtin' her an' if you're fond of her, tell her I'll be fond of her too.

*(Exit Daigan.)*

**Padraic**
Can you hear me, Nellie? ... I'm tellin' you that I care for you ... I really care for you ... I feel so deeply for you that words are a waste. I know myself and I know that you're the woman for me. That's all I can tell you for now and it's the only way I know how to tell you. Would you marry me soon an' come back to Clare with me? *(He goes near her and puts his hands on her shoulders, she is still turned away from him.)* You'll like it over in Cuas an' you'll be happy because I'll make you happy an' I'll work mornin', noon an' night for your happiness.

*(Slowly Nellie turns and faces him.)*

**Nellie**
No Padraic. It's no good.... You don't love me.... Go back to Clare and marry a good-lookin' girl that you might have real passion for. It's some kind of pity you feel, and pity is not what I want an' it wouldn't be any good for you either. Take your stuff an' go now because I'm goin' to cry in a minute an' I'll be a terrible sight because there's that many years o' tears inside o' me I'd frighten you an' I don't want you to go away with greater pity for me.

**Padraic**
What am I goin' to say to you or what honest way can a man express himself when he wants to pour out the real feelings of his heart? I can't say I love you. I wouldn't understand what I'd be saying myself if I did.

**Nellie**
Say no more only go now, because every word you say is hurtin' me more an' more

an' if you don't go quick I'll have to run away an' hide myself. I'm serious too an' I can't listen to you any more. Go, go on away to the boat an' don't have the neighbours laughin' at me, so if you have any small spatter of the compassion you say you have you'll turn on your heel an' go out that door now this minute.

**Padraic**  If I said Nellie, 'I love you', it would mean only three words. Anyone can say them. Anyone can say 'I love you' ... I can't. It would mean nothin' to me but I know I can give you a lifetime of labour an' I'll give you the strength o' my shoulders and my body an' all the power that's in me to cater for you, Nellie Brick. I don't know whether that's love or not but that's what I want to do for you. *(Lifts her aloft.)* I want to twirl you like a spinning top and stop you from spinning slowly, to know every bit of you.

**Nellie**  You mean it Padraic ... you really mean it?

**Padraic**  I never felt for anyone what I feel for you. It's broken in me whatever it was that damned up my natural feelings.

*(They embrace.)*

**Nellie**  O, Padraic, my Padraic ... my dear, dear Padraic. What will we do, what will I do about you?

**Padraic**  I'll come for you at the first low tide in September an' we'll be married. I can't do anything before that because I have to settle a pile of things first, in Cuas.

**Nellie**  I'll be waitin' for you at the low tide.

*(They embrace again.)*

**Padraic**

Do you know the pier at Cuas? Did you ever spot it across the water?

**Nellie**

I often saw it of a fine mornin'.

*(Padraic puts his hands around her waist and they stand in the doorway.)*

**Padraic**

Look, *(Points)* look now apast my hand, well to the left. It's the third whitewashed house over the harbour to the sea side of the pier. Do you see it?

**Nellie**

Is that it! I often noticed that house when I was a child and I wondered what kind of strange people lived there.

**Padraic**

I used to look across here often when I was young in summertime, an' there used to be a blue haze mindin' the low hills here at this side o' the Shannon. Did you ever feel a great loneliness when you see a crooked wall of low hills in the distance and silver so plentiful on the water between, that there wouldn't be any cure for your loneliness unless there was someone you could tell your feelin's to?

**Nellie**

I know ... I know better than anybody.... Oh, look at them two, it's Pakey and Petey an' what's that they have between them? He's like he'd be dead an' here's the crowd from the boat followin' them.

**Padraic**

*(Joining Nellie in laughter)* That's Cooney, the corner forward.

**Nellie**

Is he drunk or what?

*(They withdraw into the kitchen from the doorway.)*

**Padraic**

I'll be off with them shortly. 'Twon't be long, a few weeks an' I'll be back.

*(Sound of music comes nearer—Pakey and Petey enter, supporting Cooney.)*

**Pakey**

High and low we searched, hither and over. At first we thought he was drowned but then we heard the snores.

**Petey**

He's still sound.... We found him asleep in a boggy field in the middle of a herd o' donkeys.

*(Pakey intones like donkey into Cooney's ear, who sleeps on undisturbed. Enter Frank followed by Daigan, Jim and others.)*

**Frank**

We're all here now. Come on down to the boat let ye! We'll march down to the boat the same as if we were never beaten.

**Cooney**

We'll rise again.

*(Enter Morisheen.)*

**Morisheen**

'Twill be our turn to cross to Clare next year.

**Pakey**

We'll give ye a hot reception.

**Petey**

We'll murder 'em!

**Pakey**

Glory Cuas!

**Petey**

Down with Bealabawn!

*(Frank, after an initial note, breaks into a march.)*

Padraic          Morisheen ... the next time you'll see me,
                 I'll be wanting the hand of your daughter.

Morisheen        *(Aloud jubilantly)* I always knew it! I always
                 knew it! 'A man with grey hair will be
                 hailed along the four shores of Ireland.
                 This man will come into his own after
                 years of torment and misery. This man will
                 have the heart of a cock blackbird for he
                 shall sit on the crown of a sidecar in the
                 streets of Killarney. A woman with a
                 supple frame an' a shinin' eye will ride by
                 his side and break the heart of a certain
                 postman in Cockatoo Lane. His son will
                 rise up to coward the country. This man
                 will be pampered and spoiled by the
                 woman of his choosing and, lo and behold,
                 the name of this man shall by Morisheen
                 Brick'. *(Swings his thumbs around and
                 points to himself.)*

                 *(All cheer and applaud.)*

Padraic          Your prophecy came true in the end,
                 Morisheen Brick. Thank God for that.

Nellie           *(Takes Padraic's hand)* The first low tide in
                 September.

Padraic          The first low tide.

Morisheen        You brought nothing but goodness here;
                 may God go with you my lovely man from
                 Clare! May God go with you all!

                 *(Meanwhile all the Clare footballers have
                 gathered at either side of the banner. At Dai-
                 gan's command they mark time, including
                 Cooney. Then, marching time slowly, they
                 sing.)*

**Footballers**

Alas now for the men of Cuas
Again we've lost the fray
Though hopes are dashed and fortunes
    crashed
We'll fight another day
Cuas men crossed, Cuas men tossed
It matters not who won or lost
Cuas, Cuas, Cuas,
Cuas, Cuas, Cuas,
What matters is to play the game.

*(Then the marching of time ceases. They stand erect. Padraic kisses Nellie farewell and marches away with the team as all sing.)*

**All**

Steady now the men of Cuas
Before the breaking day
Our tide is high, a last goodbye
Before we sail away
Cuas boys here, Cuas boys there
Cuas boys, Cuas boys everywhere
Cuas, Cuas, Cuas,
Cuas, Cuas, Cuas,
The men of Cuas are always there.

# Final Curtain

# The Men of Cuas

Words and music: John B. Keane
Arrangement: James N. Healy

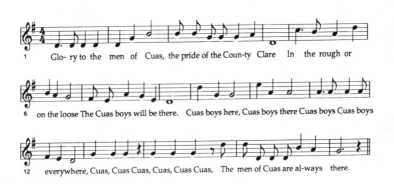

1  Glo- ry to the men of Cuas, the pride of the Coun-ty Clare  In the rough or

6  on the loose The Cuas boys will be there.  Cuas boys here, Cuas boys there Cuas boys Cuas boys

12  everywhere, Cuas, Cuas Cuas, Cuas, Cuas Cuas,  The men of Cuas are al-ways  there.

## The Men of Cuas

Glory to the men of Cuas
The pride of the County Clare
In the rough or on the loose
The Cuas boys will be there.
Cuas boys here, Cuas boys there
Cuas boys, Cuas boys everywhere.
Cuas, Cuas, Cuas,
Cuas, Cuas, Cuas,
The men of Cuas are always there.

# *More Plays from Mercier*

## THE FIELD

### John B. Keane

THE FIELD is John B. Keane's fierce and tender study of the love a man can have for land and the ruthless lengths to which he will go in order to obtain the object of his desire. *Now a major film.*

\*\*\*

## THE YEAR OF THE HIKER

### John B. Keane

The Hiker is the much hated father who deserted his wife and family and whose return is awaited with fear.

\*\*\*

## MOLL

### John B. Keane

MOLL is John B. Keane's hilarious and highly successful comedy about life in an Irish country presbytery.

# THE BUDS OF BALLYBUNION

## John B. Keane

The Buds come to the seaside at Ballybunion for their yearly break. (Bud is the abbreviation of the Irish word, *bodaire*, meaning a rough country person.)

*** 

# THE CHASTITUTE

## John B. Keane

'A Chastitute is a person without holy orders who has never lain down with a woman.' This is the definition given by John B. Keane, who in this amusing play holds up some 'sacred cows' to ridicule.

*** 

# THE CHANGE IN MAME FADDEN

## John B. Keane

A powerful drama depicting a woman facing the change of life, and how her family fail to understand the turmoil she is experiencing.

# THE CRAZY WALL

## John B. Keane

An amusing play that holds some 'sacred cows' up to ridicule.

*** 

# VALUES

## John B. Keane

Three one-act plays: *The Spraying of John O'Dorey, Backwater* and *The Pure of Heart.*

***

# THREE PLAYS:
## Sive, The Field, Big Maggie

## John B. Keane

*Sive* is a powerful folk-drama which concerns itself with a cynical attempt to sell an innocent girl to a lecherous old man; *The Field* deals with the social and moral effects of land greed; *Big Maggie* is about the domination of a family by a tyrannical mother.

# *Bestselling Fiction from Mercier*

## DURANGO

### John B. Keane

An adventure story about life in rural Ireland during the Second World War. Set in an Ireland that is fast dying, John B. Keane, with his wonderful skill and humour, brings it to life in this novel, rekindling in the reader memories of a time never to be quite forgotten....

\*\*\*

## THE RAM OF GOD
### and Other Stories

### John B. Keane

A collection of fascinating and hilarious stories from the pen of one of Ireland's most popular writers. Who can resist John B. Keane on 'Is Cork Sinking?', 'Fear', 'Weird but Normal', 'English Words but the Accent is Irish', 'Drunken Man', 'Proverbs', and 'Illusions of Grandeur'?

\*\*\*